Blackstone's Guide to
Landlord and Tenant Covenants:
The New Law in Practice

BLACKSTONE'S GUIDE TO

Landlord and Tenant Covenants:
The New Law in Practice

Professor Phillip H. Kenny
LLB, Dip Crim LLM, Solicitor

Head of School of Law, University of Northumbria
at Newcastle

and

Russell Hewitson
LLB, PGCED, Solicitor

Senior Lecturer in Law, School of Law, University
of Northumbria at Newcastle

BLACKSTONE
PRESS LIMITED

First published in Great Britain 1996 by Blackstone Press Limited,
9-15 Aldine Street, London W12 8AW.   Telephone 0181-740 1173

ISBN: 1 85431 487 4

British Library Cataloguing in Publication Data
A CIP catalogue record for this book is available from the British Library.

Typeset by Style Photosetting Limited, Mayfield, East Sussex
Printed by Livesey Limited, Shrewsbury, Shropshire

Contents

covenants — Overriding leases — Lease renewals — Rent review —
Incorporation of the statutory disregards — Rent deposit bonds — The
Tyneside Flat Scheme — Registered Conveyancing New Rules

Preface

This book deals with changes in landlord and tenant law which have a great significance, particularly for commercial conveyancing practice.

We provide a detailed analysis of the Landlord and Tenant (Covenants) Act 1995 in chapter 2, followed by a discussion of points of especial practical significance. The full text of the Act is given in appendix 1.

Precedents are given in appendix 4. The question whether the modern commercial lease will survive in its present shape and length will be decided more by market forces than by the intricacies of the legislation.

We have tried to state the old law where it is relevant as it was immediately before the Act came into force on 1 January 1996.

P. H. Kenny
R. Hewitson
Newcastle-upon-Tyne
30 January 1996

Abbreviations

1995 Act	Landlord and Tenant (Covenants) Act 1995
AGA	authorised guarantee agreement
LPA 1925	Law of Property Act 1925

1

Summary of the 1995 Act

The Landlord and Tenant (Covenants) Act 1995 started life as a private member's Bill and with little debate it was eventually passed into law with all-party support. Unusually for a law reform Bill it does not have a useful history of government discussion papers or Law Commission working papers. In 1988 the Law Commission produced a report, *Landlord and Tenant Law: Privity of Contract and Estate* (Law Com No. 174), which recommended the abolition of the privity of contract rule under which a landlord and tenant continue to be liable to each other under their lease after assigning it. The Commission proposed that this change should apply to existing and new leases alike. Unfortunately the Law Commission paper is of little value in the interpretation of the 1995 Act.

The overall effect of the Act is to replace the existing law of privity of estate and privity of contract with a new set of rules. These new rules apply to new tenancies only, so for all lawyers practising in the future (until every lease granted before 1996 has disappeared) there will be two sets of rules: the old rules for old tenancies and the new rules for new tenancies. With a new tenancy the tenant will on assignment be released from the tenant covenants in the lease. A landlord on assignment will be able also to obtain release from the landlord covenants. To counterbalance the end of privity of contract for tenants there are new rules on consent for assignment and a new form of guarantee (the authorised guarantee agreement) which may be extracted from an assigning tenant. The Act contains important new rules restricting the recovery of rent arrears from former tenants. A former tenant who has to pay such arrears may obtain an overriding lease (s. 19) so as to assume the position of landlord in respect of the defaulting tenant. Changes are also made to the consequences for former tenants and guarantors of variation in a lease.

Little help in interpreting the final Act can be found from the Parliamentary debates. It was discussed in Parliament as follows:

Commons	*Lords*
1st reading 14 February 1995	1st reading 24 April 1995
2nd reading 21 April 1995	2nd reading 25 April 1995
3rd reading 21 April 1995	3rd reading 12 July 1995

The Act received Royal Assent on 19 July 1995 and is in force from 1 January 1996.

The following is a summary of its main effects.

Section 1 is preliminary and describes the tenancies to which the Act applies.

Section 2 is preliminary and describes the covenants to which the Act applies.

Provisions applying only to post-1995 leases

Transmission of benefit and burden

Sections 3 and 4 provide for the benefit and burden of covenants and rights of re-entry to run with the lease and reversion.

The Act abolishes privity of contract for all new leases after 31 December 1995. This means that on assignment the tenant is automatically released.

If the assignment is in breach of covenant or by operation of law then this effect is delayed until the next assignment (s. 11).

The assignee is, from assignment, liable on all covenants in the lease except any which are expressed to be personal (s. 3(6)(a)). The concept of covenants which 'touch and concern the land' thus disappears for new leases.

It is possible for a landlord to be released on assignment of the reversion (s. 7). This requires a set procedure to be followed. The procedure is set out in s. 8. Notice is given to the tenant. If the tenant then objects the question of whether the landlord is released is decided by the court if the landlord applies. The Act states no criteria for the court to apply in coming to its decision and presumably it will depend on whether the assignee is able and likely to perform the landlord's obligations.

Where there is an assignment of part of the land in a lease then:

(a) The assignor and the assignee are each liable on covenants *attributable* to their parts. Section 9(6) provides that non-attributable means not falling to be complied with in relation to any premises comprised in the assignment.

(b) In respect of non-attributable covenants liability should be apportioned. This will be done by agreement between the assignor and the assignee. The apportionment may become binding on other parties, e.g., the landord if the procedure under s. 10 is used. This requires first of all a notice to be served on that party. If that party objects, the issue will be decided by the county court if the assignor and assignee apply.

Covenants with management companies

Section 12 is intended to ensure that an assignee can enforce covenants by third parties such as management companies.

Authorised guarantee agreement

Section 16 permits an assignor to be forced to enter an authorised guarantee agreement (AGA) guaranteeing the performance of the assignee. This can be done if:

(a) consent is needed for the assignment, and

(b) such consent is given subject to a condition (lawfully imposed) that the assignor will enter into an AGA.

Provisions which apply to all leases

In respect of all leases a former tenant who is liable for arrears must be given notice of such arrears within six months of them becoming due (s. 17).

Variation of tenancies

Presently the common law effect of variation of a lease by an assignee and the landlord is very problematical. The variation is likely to discharge the original tenant's guarantor. Its effect on the original tenant has been unclear. Now s. 18 has specific provisions which apply to all leases (see s. 18(2) and (3)). The effect is:

(a)   The former tenant and the guarantor remain liable for increased rent due to operation of the rent provisions provided the terms of the provisions are not varied.

(b)   Where the covenants are varied a former tenant is not liable to pay any increase resulting from the variation (s. 18(2)).

(c)   If there is a variation which could prejudice a guarantor the guarantor is discharged at common law (*Holme* v *Brunskill* (1877) 3 QBD 495).

(d)   In any event the guarantor is not liable for any increase in liability caused by a variation of covenants in the lease (s. 18(3)).

Use of overriding leases

An overriding lease is one granted by the landlord for a longer term than the existing lease in respect of which it is an overriding lease. Under s. 19 a former tenant who is called upon to pay for a subsequent assignee's liability may call for an overriding lease. With a new lease this will apply only to a former tenant who is bound by an AGA.

Other provisions

Forfeiture or disclaimer of part (new leases only)

Where a tenant following assignment is a tenant only of part then forfeiture and disclaimer will operate only in respect of that part.

Landlord's consent to assignments (new leases only)

Section 22 is a very important section which amends the Landlord and Tenant Act 1927) s. 19. This allows advance specification of the circumstances in which consent to assignment is to be withheld. It also amends the Landlord and Tenant Act 1988, s. 1, to the same effect. Such agreements can be entered into at any time even after a lease has been granted.

No contracting out

Section 25 prevents contracting out of the Act and applies to new and old leases and to agreements made before the Act came into force.

Amendment of the Landlord and Tenant Act 1954, s. 34

The provisions of the 1995 Act are to be taken into account in calculating the rent on a statutory renewal under the 1954 Act.

Amendment of the Landlord and Tenant Act 1954, s. 35

The provisions of the 1995 Act are to be taken into account in settling the other terms of a renewal lease.

2

The 1995 Act Section by Section

Section 1 Tenancies to which the Act applies

The most important provisions of the 1995 Act apply only to new tenancies. For the purposes of the Act a new tenancy is one which is granted on or after 1 January 1996. A tenancy is granted on the beginning of the day on which it is effectively executed. This means that the Act cannot be avoided by backdating a deed executed after 1995 nor by stating in the deed a date for commencement earlier than the date for execution (see, e.g., *Jayne* v *Hughes* (1854) 10 Ex 430 at p. 433). New tenancies do not include those granted pursuant to an agreement entered into before 1 January 1996 or pursuant to a court order made before that date (s. 1(3)). In order to prevent future disputes about whether such a lease is or is not a new tenancy, such a lease should include a statement to the effect that it is not a new tenancy (see appendix 4). It appears that renewal leases under the Landlord and Tenant Act 1954, Part II, will be new leases even where proceedings were commenced before 1996 and are still continuing.

The 1995 Act also makes it clear that a tenancy granted pursuant to an option entered into before 1 January 1996 is not a new tenancy (s. 1(6)). Section 1(7) contains the remarkable provision that 'In subsection (6) "option" includes the right of first refusal'. This was meant to include within the definition of an 'option' rights of pre-emption which are quite clearly not 'options' within the proper meaning of that term. A right of pre-emption is the right to be offered the chance to purchase an interest in property when the owner wishes to market it. It may, obviously, be a right to be offered the second or third or other refusal not necessarily the first. Though the point may never arise the court can avoid the effect of this patent error in drafting by reading 'first' adverbially rather than adjectivally. It, then, should read the right of refusal first — that is, the right of refusal before the property is offered openly. Tenancies created under all such rights granted before 1996 will then fall outside the definition of new tenancy in s. 1(3).

A more difficult provision to apply precisely is s. 1(5). A fresh tenancy can arise by deemed surrender and regrant where there is a variation of an existing tenancy. Section 1(5) provides that if this occurs after 31 December 1995 there is a *new tenancy* within s. 1(3) of the Act. This issue has arisen recently in *Friends Provident Life Office* v *British Railways Board* [1995] 48 EG 106. The landlord and assignee agreed variations in the rent and assignment covenant. This did not cause a surrender and regrant. The court reviewing the authorities thought there were probably only two cases where there would be an implied surrender and regrant — that is, where the amount of property in the lease is increased or the term of the lease is extended. This case law is discussed further at pages 35–39.

Section 2   Covenants to which the Act applies

Introduction

The purpose of the 1995 Act is that a tenant who assigns is to be relieved from the burden of the tenant 'covenants of the tenancy' and can no longer enjoy the landlord 'covenants of the tenancy'. The Act is applied by s. 2 to all landlord and tenant covenants 'of a tenancy'. Sometimes the original tenant under a lease has obligations which are not undertaken in the role of tenant as such and which it is intended should survive any assignment. For example, the tenant may agree to provide for a period of years a commercial service for the landlord or pay a commission on goods sold or accept a restriction on his own trade. Where the tenancy is assigned during that period of years, what is the consequence for this collateral part of the bargain? Are these obligations covenants of the tenancy?

Section 2(1)   Covenant of a tenancy

The expression 'covenant of a tenancy' is not clear in its meaning. Does it necessarily include all the obligations included in a written lease whether or not they are concerned with the subject matter of the demise? Section 2(1)(a) discussed below provides clearly that it does. On the other hand the question arises whether it can include obligations not in the written lease but in collateral documentation. In view of the express provisions of s. 2(1) it would seem the better view that the Act applies to all obligations which are included or incorporated in any way in the tenancy agreement. Section 28(1) takes the matter even further by providing that 'covenant of a tenancy' includes terms 'in a collateral agreement' and that 'collateral agreement' includes agreements made before or after the lease. The only area of doubt concerns how an agreement has to be linked to a tenancy in order to be 'collateral' to it.

Is it a covenant?

It may be necessary to determine whether an obligation is a covenant. An example is *Paterson* v *Aggio* (1987) 19 HLR 551, CA. This suggests that where a forfeiture clause in common form allows forfeiture on the grounds of various insolvency events this imposes an *obligation* on the tenant not to incur such an insolvency event.

Section 2(1)(a)   Covenant need not 'touch and concern the land'

Section 2 contains a radical change in the definition of landlord and tenant covenants. Section 2(1)(a) states that the Act applies to a covenant 'whether or not the covenant has reference to the subject matter of the tenancy'. Thus, in relation to new tenancies, all the nice decisions on whether a covenant 'touches and concerns the land' are swept into oblivion. The covenant has, though, to be a covenant 'of a tenancy', a concept which has already been discussed.

Section 2(1)(b)   Act applies to express and implied covenants

Section 2(1)(b) further provides that the Act applies to a covenant 'whether the covenant is express, implied or imposed by law'. Thus, the benefit of the landlord's covenants implied by the Landlord and Tenant Act 1985, s. 11, are dealt with in the same way as express covenants.

Personal covenants

Lest it be argued that neither 'landlord covenant' nor 'tenant covenant' includes covenants expressed to be personal, s. 28(1) provides that:

(a) 'landlord covenant', in relation to a tenancy, means a covenant falling to be complied with by the landlord of premises demised by the tenancy;

(b) 'tenant covenant', in relation to a tenancy, means a covenant falling to be complied with by the tenant of premises demised by the tenancy.

A personal covenant does not fall to be complied with by the tenant qua tenant. However, this is precisely what is no longer required to make a covenant a tenant covenant. What is required simply is that the covenant is *in fact* entered into by the tenant with the landlord (and similarly with landlord covenants). And all that is required of any provisions in order to fall within the Act is that they are something to do with the lease in that they must be in the lease or in a collateral agreement. In this context, collateral must simply mean 'something to do with'. The expression 'falling to be complied with' by the tenant or the landlord — as the case may be — must simply mean having in fact to be complied with. The simple fact that a covenant has to be performed by the person who is in fact the landlord or the tenant makes the covenant a landlord or a tenant covenant.

Personal covenants are then dealt with as special cases in various parts of the Act as follows:

(a) by s. 3(6)(a), covenants which are expressed to be personal are not to be enforceable against a successor;

(b) by s. 19(3), personal covenants are not to be included in an overriding lease.

Section 2(2)   Certain excepted covenants

A number of particular covenants imposed by housing legislation are specifically excepted from the Act:

(a)   The covenant under the Housing Act 1985, s. 35. This is the covenant to repay a discount given on a voluntary disposal by a local authority under s. 32 of that Act.

(b)   The covenant under the Housing Act 1985, s. 155. This is the covenant to repay a discount given on exercise of the right to buy under that Act.

(c)   The covenant under the Housing Act 1985, sch. 6A, para. 1. This is a covenant to redeem the landlord's share where the right to buy on rent to mortgage terms has been exercised.

(d)   The covenants under the Housing Associations Act 1985, sch. 2, paras 1 and 3. These provisions apply to repayments of discount or restrictions on disposal of housing association properties sold at a discount or disposed of in National Parks, areas of outstanding natural beauty or certain other designated rural areas.

Section 3   Transmission of covenants

Section 3(1) is the boiler room of the legislation. It provides that the benefit and burden of all landlord and tenant covenants as defined in s. 2 pass to an assignee on an assignment of the lease or the reversion.

Annexation is expressed to be to the whole and to each and every part of the demised premises and of the reversion. Without s. 3(2) this could produce a patently absurd result where there is an assignment of part of the land in a lease. If a landlord lets six shops to a tenant who then assigns each to a different person the whole of the covenants would be 'annexed and incident' to each shop and the tenant of shop six could be brought to task for the failures of the tenant of shop one. This result is avoided by s. 3(2), which provides that the tenant becomes bound 'from the assignment'. The tenant is not, however, bound by covenants that 'immediately before the assignment . . . did not bind the assignor' (s. 3(2)(a)(i)). If a release from a particular covenant has been given to the tenant then the assignee from that tenant will similarly not be bound. This may come as a surprise to the landlord if the release was intended to be personal (see s. 3(4) below). Secondly the assignee is not bound by the obligation to the extent that it falls 'to be complied with in relation to any demised premises not comprised in the assignment' (s. 3(2)(a)(ii)). Thus, in the example just given the covenant to use shop one as a butcher's does not burden the assignee of shop six.

By s. 3(3), these rules apply to assignments by the landlord in the same way as to tenant assignments.

Waivers and releases

Under s. 3(2) and (3), an assignee of a landlord or a tenant is not bound by a covenant to the extent that it is not binding upon the assignor. Section 3(4) applies to any waiver or release given to such an assignor. It provides that any waiver or release given to the assignor is disregarded if it is '(in whatever terms) . . . expressed to be personal to the assignor'. This form of words has two important consequences:

(a) It is only an *express* waiver or release which is disregarded. One arising by estoppel is not disregarded by this provision.

(b) It is not a question of whether the waiver or release was intended to be personal but whether it was expressed to be. Thus to ensure s. 3(4) operates, transparently clear provisions are needed.

not sure about
this — prob. just take
at face value — applied to
occupiers

Section 3(5)   Restrictive covenants

Section 3(5) provides that a restrictive covenant is capable of being enforced against any owner or occupier of demised premises to which the covenant relates. A restrictive covenant which is binding upon the landlord's estate must be complied with in any event by such persons — see *Re Nisbet and Potts' Contract* [1906] 1 Ch 386. Section 3(5) is concerned with covenants in the tenancy agreement. These generally do not bind other occupiers at common law because their effectiveness depends on the privity of estate between tenant and landlord (see *Tichborne* v *Weir* (1892) 67 LT 735) although there is no reason why such a covenant may not in fact satisfy the requirements for a restrictive covenant to be enforceable in equity and as such not bind any other occupiers under the doctrine of *Re Nisbet and Potts' Contract.*

The curious wording of s. 3(5) refers to a restriction being *capable* of being enforced even though there is no express provision in the tenancy to that effect. This wording does nothing more than make up for the fact that the LPA 1925, s. 79, does not apply to new tenancies (see s. 30(4)(a) of the 1995 Act). The net result is that a covenant within s. 3(5) is enforceable against an owner or occupier of premises to which it relates only if it could have been enforced under an express provision of the tenancy.

To take an example, a covenant not to use premises except as a butcher's shop can be enforced against an owner or occupier of the premises as if it said: 'The tenant covenants not to use the premises except as a butcher's shop and this covenant is deemed to be given by any owner or occupier of the demised premises'. However, unless an owner or occupier is bound by privity of contract or is an assignee, the covenant will still be unenforceable unless it satisfies the requirements for enforcement in equity as a restrictive covenant.

The commentary on this provision in *Current Law Statutes Annotated* states, 'This subsection . . . contains an important extension of the enforceability of user covenants in a tenancy, which may be very significant for estate management by landlords'. This is not so. The same conditions for enforcement are required as under the previous law. The only substantive provision of s. 3(5) is that the application of the covenant to other occupiers need not be mentioned. To return to the covenant not to use the shop except as a butcher's shop, this would be enforceable against a squatter only by a landlord who is within the rules in *Tulk* v *Moxhay* (1842) 2 Ph 774 for enforcing restrictive covenants.

Section 3(6)(a)   Personal covenants

Section 3(6)(a) applies to a covenant which '(in whatever terms) is expressed to be personal'. An example will explain the effect. Suppose the tenant promises 'as a personal covenant to keep the demised premises open for business as a reputable solicitor's office'. Upon assignment this covenant ceases to bind the covenanting tenant (s. 5(2)). The effect of s. 3(6)(a) is that s. 3 will not make the covenant binding on the assignee either.

An important consequence of this is that covenants which are intended to be personal should be expressed to be personal so that they do not inadvertently bind assignees.

Section 3(6)(b)   Need for registration

Covenants in leases which required registration under the Land Charges Act 1972 or the Land Registration Act 1925 still require such registration if they are now to be fully enforceable. The position is as follows.

Unregistered land   Restrictive covenants in leases are expressly exempted from the need for registration (Land Charges Act 1972, s. 2(5)(ii)). Estate contracts contained in leases require registration (as Class C (iv) land charges). If they are not registered then they will not bind a purchaser for money or money's worth of the reversion or a legal estate carved out of it (Land Charges Act 1972, s. 4(6)). Section 3(6)(b) of the 1995 Act provides in effect that this rule survives the new Act. The other not uncommon interest requiring registration contained in a lease is an equitable easement (Class D(iii) land charge).

Registered land   If the tenancy is carved out of a registered estate then the lease will be automatically noted against the title out of which it is created.

If the tenancy is created out of unregistered estate then a land charge which requires protection in the case of unregistered land must be registered against the estate owner in the circumstances described for unregistered land above.

Section 3(7)   Covenants concerning subject matter not yet in existence

Section 3(7) refers to an ancient common law rule. An obligation upon the tenant to do 'some entirely new thing' (Megarry and Wade, *The Law of Real Property*, 5th ed. (1984), p. 750) ran with the burdened land only if assignees were expressly mentioned. The rule derived from *Spencer's Case* (1583) 5 Co Rep 16a of which Sir Edward Coke said:

> ... if the lessee had covenanted for him and his assignees, that they would make a new wall on some part of the thing demised, that for as much as it is to be done upon the land demised, that it should bind the assignee; for although the covenant doth extend to a thing to be newly made, yet it is to be made upon the thing demised, and the assignee is to take the benefit of it, and therefore [it] shall bind the assignee by express words.

The rule was clearly intended to be abolished by the LPA 1925, s. 79(1), which provides: 'This subsection extends to a covenant to do some act relating to the land, notwithstanding that the subject matter may not be in existence when the covenant is made'. However, s. 79 does not apply to new leases — see s. 30(4)(a) of the 1995 Act. There are now the following possibilities in relation to a tenant's covenant to do some entirely new thing:

(a)   Covenants in leases made before 1926. These are subject to the ancient rule and are not affected by s. 3(7) which applies only to new tenancies.

(b)   Covenants in leases made on or after 1 January 1926 but before 1 January 1996. These are subject to the LPA 1925 and will bind assignees unless a contrary intention is expressed.

(c)   Covenants in leases made after 1995. The ancient common law rule is abolished. Under the 1995 Act covenants run whether or not they are personal and whether or not assignees are mentioned.

There is in the 1995 Act a definition of assignment (s. 28(1)). It provides that assignment includes an equitable assignment, assignments in breach of a covenant of the tenancy or assignments by operation of law. The question of how the Act applies to different assignments is dealt with fully in the commentary below on s. 11, which deals with 'excluded assignments'.

Section 4   Transmission of right of re-entry

In respect of old leases the benefit of a landlord's right of re-entry ran with the reversion by virtue of the LPA 1925, s. 141. This is so notwithstanding a severance of the reversion — see the LPA 1925, s. 140. The LPA 1925, s. 141, does not apply to a new leases — see s. 30(4)(b) of the 1995 Act —

but new leases are covered by s. 4 of the 1995 Act which is to the same effect.

Section 5   Release on assignment

The purpose of s. 5 is to achieve the desired effect of removing the privity of contract rule from landlord and tenant law.

Section 5(1) describes the scope of the Act quite wrongly. It says, 'This section applies where a tenant assigns premises demised to him under a tenancy'. However, the section will clearly be applied where the assignment happens by operation of law and not by an act of the tenant. Equally clearly it applies not only when the property has been demised to the assigning tenant but simply where at the time of the assignment it is held by the assigning tenant. Thus, 'demised' in this context clearly means 'presently demised'. The aim of the Act to apply in the wider circumstances described is perfectly clear from the definition of assignment in s. 28 and the manifest absurdity which would result if the literal wording of the Act was followed. The way the Act applies to different kinds of 'assignments' (as defined by s. 28) is discussed in the commentary on s. 11 below.

Section 5(2)   Assignment by tenant — transmission

Section 5(2) provides for the automatic release of the tenant on assignment of the whole. The tenant is released from the tenant covenants and ceases to be entitled to the benefit of the landlord covenants.

Section 5(2) states the effect where the assignment is *by the tenant.* To make sense of the provisions this will be read as assignments *from the tenant* because otherwise it would exclude assignments which occur by operation of law. These, as s. 28(1) and (6) show beyond doubt, are intended to be within the scope of the Act although they fall to be treated as excluded assignments under s. 11 (see below). Section 28(6) provides that in the case of both a landlord and a tenant an assignment means any transfer from the landlord or tenant as the case may be.

The effect of s. 5(2) is that from the date of an assignment the tenant is automatically released from tenant covenants and can no longer benefit from landlord covenants.

The curious effect seems to be that a tenant is released from any purely personal covenants which the tenant can persuade the court are 'covenants of a tenancy' within s. 2 of the 1995 Act. The sweeping effect of the definition of a tenant covenant in s. 2(1) is so great that personal covenants by the tenant which are intended to survive assignment cannot be included in tenancy agreements. When it is desired to obtain such covenants from a tenant, an agreement must be made entirely separate from the tenancy. This conclusion could have been avoided if the Act had said that a 'tenant covenant' does not include a covenant which is expressed to be a personal covenant so as to fall within s. 3(6) of the Act. (On the definition of a tenant covenant see the commentary on s. 2 above.) Where a landlord and tenant enter into a commercial agreement it may be helpful to provide that, 'This agreement is (or is not) collateral to the tenancy and is personal to the tenant'.

Section 5(3)   Release of tenant on assignment of part

When a tenant assigns part of the premises in a lease then the release operates only to the extent that the covenants fall to be complied with in relation to that part. The tenant who assigns remains liable in respect of covenants which do not apply to any particular part of the property or which apply to parts which are not assigned. The way this works is considered further in the commentary on s. 9 which deals with the apportionment of liability between tenant and assignee. If there is no apportionment then both are jointly and severally liable on covenants which do not apply to particular parts of the premises (see s. 13(1)).

Section 5(4)

This provides that s. 5 operates whether or not the tenant is currently the tenant of the whole of the property in the tenancy. So s. 5 will apply when an assigning tenant has already assigned a part of the property.

Sections 6 to 8   Release of landlord on assignment of reversion

Presumably out of some idea of fairness to the landlord, ss. 6 to 8 create the possibility of the landlord being released from the landlord's covenants on an assignment of the reversion. As is the case with assignments by a tenant, s. 28(6) makes it clear that assignment means any transfer from the landlord however effected and whether or not by the landlord. The reason given in Parliament for the more cumbersome procedure for landlord release is this. Landlords have the power to control assignment by tenants. Tenants have no such control over their landlords. The role of the court in controlling release of assignor landlords to some extent redresses this balance.

It will be noted that by s. 3 the benefit and burden of landlord's covenants pass to an assignee of the reversion. *Such an assignee now remains liable unless released under ss. 6 to 8.*

The procedure for release of a landlord looks cumbersome but nevertheless its frequent use, particularly by large-scale property companies, may be anticipated. Readers of great antiquity will remember the coming into force in 1970 of the Law of Property Act 1969, s. 5, which allowed applications to opt out of the business tenancies code and seemed at first to require cumbersome court proceedings but now has become one of the most routine of formalities.

There are good commercial reasons for taking advantage of this measure. A company which diverts itself of a portfolio of reversionary interests will be anxious to remove from its books the contingent liability it has as the original landlord. Any solicitor acting for the assignor of a reversion must advise the client of the procedures available to it to be released from liability, so that it is in a position to make an informed decision.

Section 6   Release of landlord

These provisions do not apply to excluded assignments — see the commentary on s. 11 below.

In order to be released from the burden of landlord covenants the landlord must apply to do so using the procedure in s. 8. A landlord who is released from landlord covenants loses the benefit of the tenant covenants (s. 6(2)(b)).

Section 6(3) applies these principles to an assignment of part of the premises. The landlord can apply under s. 8 to be released from the landlord covenants 'to the extent that they fall to be complied with in relation to that part of those premises'. If the landlord is so released then it ceases to be able to enforce the tenant covenants 'only to the extent that they fall to be complied with in relation to that part of the premises'.

These provisions may have a curious effect. Suppose a block of offices has tenants T1 to T20. T1 to T10 are the tenants of the top half and T11 to T20 of the bottom half. Suppose the lease of the top half included the roof and that the landlord is under an obligation to all tenants to maintain that roof and to pay the cost annually. If the landlord assigns the top half then under s. 8 the landlord may be released from the covenant only in respect of obligations to T1 to T10 (see s. 8(4)(a) definition of 'tenant' for these purposes). Under s. 6(3)(b) presumably the landlord only loses the benefit of covenants in respect of which it is released from the burden. If a landlord were released under these provisions from liability to T1 to T10 it would retain its obligations (and rights) against T11 to T20. If that is the correct interpretation of these provisions then the court might be reluctant to release the landlord under s. 8. It appears fairly clear that there is a separate possibility of release in respect of each tenant when the reversion is assigned. This rather odd effect occurs where the landlord is under an obligation to repair a part which benefits tenants generally but is not demised to all of them.

Section 6(4)   Landlord of part

Section 6(4) provides that the procedures for landlord release from covenants apply in cases where the landlord is not the landlord of the whole of the premises in which the reversion is assigned. Such a case is when the landlord has already assigned a part of the reversion.

Section 7   Release of former landlord

Section 7 allows for the release of a former landlord of premises on a subsequent assignment of the reversion. The former landlord may use the procedure under s. 8 to be released from the benefit and burden of covenants to which it is still subject. A former landlord of only part of the premises in a tenancy can be released only to the extent that a covenant 'falls to be complied with in relation to any premises comprised in the assignment' (s. 7(3)). A former landlord who is not landlord of any other premises in the tenancy may be released from liability *in toto*. A former landlord released from liability under these provisions also loses the benefit of the covenants.

The following cases may occur:

(a)   L granted a lease of a property and assigned the whole reversion to R1. On that occasion L failed to apply for a release. R1 now assigns to R2 and L can apply under s. 7 for a complete release.

(b)   L granted a lease of property and assigned to R. L applied for release and was turned down by the court. L can apply again on R's assignment. Section 7(6)(b) makes it clear that a former landlord can apply on a subsequent assignment in any circumstances.

(c)   L granted a lease to T and assigned part to R1. On an assignment by R1, L can apply to be released from the covenants relating to that part.

(d)   L granted a lease to T and assigned part to R1 and part to R2. On an assignment by R1 or R2, L can apply to be released in respect of the whole.

Section 8   Procedure for release of landlord

A notice must be served on the tenant either before the assignment or within four weeks beginning with the assignment. The time limits are strict and there is no provision in the Act for their relaxation.

If different parts of the premises are held by different tenants then notice must be served on all of them (s. 8(4)(a)).

Time is calculated as follows. The date of the assignment is the date the assignment takes effect as an instrument or an act in law. Thus, if the assignment is by deed it is the date the deed is effectively executed. If it is delivered as an escrow the date of the deed is the date of such delivery as an escrow and not the date the condition of the escrow is satisfied. This rather odd rule appears to be consistent with the Court of Appeal decision in *Alan Estates Ltd* v *WG Stores Ltd* [1982] Ch 511, which in turn resulted from application of the doctrine of 'relation back' to escrows, but the decision is plainly wrong in its reasoning and in its historical context (see the dissenting judgment of Ackner LJ and an article in [1982] Conv 409).

No difficulty in practice need be caused by the difficulty of precisely calculating this four-week period as there is no restriction on how early the notice can be served.

The form of the notice

The forms of notice prescribed by the Lord Chancellor under s. 27(1) are reproduced in appendix 3.

Service of the notice

By s. 27(5), service of notices under s. 8 is governed by the Landlord and Tenant Act 1927, s. 23. Thus, personal service, service at the tenant's last known place of abode or service by recorded or registered post can be used. If there is an abortive assignment to one purchaser of the reversion then a fresh notice will have to be served in respect of any future assignment which the landlord negotiates.

Tenant's reply

The tenant may either accede to the landlord's release or not. The possibilities are as follows:

(a) If the tenant does not reply within four weeks of receipt of the landlord's notice then any covenant is released to the extent mentioned in the notice (s. 8(2)(a)).

(b) If the tenant does reply within four weeks objecting to the release then the landlord has to apply to the court (s. 8(2)(b)). The tenant's objection is by notice in the prescribed form which actually forms a detachable part of the landlord's notice (see appendix 3).

(c) The tenant may serve a notice consenting to the release. The tenant may do this even after serving a notice objecting to the release (s. 8(2)(c)). It might be thought that a tenant could be persuaded to serve this notice at the beginning of a lease. However, for there to be an effective notice there must be a particular assignment of which notice is given.

Landlord's application to the court

The court is the county court and it has exclusive jurisdiction (s. 8(4)(c)). The court has to decide whether 'it is reasonable for the covenant to be so released'. No criteria of reasonableness are stated in the Act. It is likely that the court's approach will centre upon the reasonableness of reliance being placed upon the new landlord's covenant. In support of such an application evidence should be led as to the financial soundness of the new landlord and, if appropriate, its track record as a landlord. It may be assumed that the evidence will be very similar to that produced to show that a tenant's assignee is a reasonable substitute for the tenant.

Section 9   Apportionment on assignment

This section is intended to assist with resolving difficulties which will arise in deciding liability on covenants where only part of the property or reversion is assigned.

The section applies only to what it calls 'non-attributable' covenants. This is a new concept and is defined by s. 9(6) as follows:

> . . . a covenant is, in relation to an assignment, a 'non-attributable' covenant if it does not fall to be complied with in relation to any premises comprised in the assignment.

This curious form of words is intended to make a distinction between the general financial commitments of the tenant and particular obligations in respect of the property. It covers, thus, the obligations to pay rent, service charges and contributions to insurance.

In respect of such covenants the section applies whenever a tenant of premises assigns part of them. It permits the tenant and the assignee to agree how the liability under the covenant is to be apportioned between them.

Agreements made between the parties to an assignment are binding only upon themselves unless the procedure under s. 10 is used to make them binding upon other persons.

Section 9(6) is amplified by s. 28(2) and (3), which explain what is meant by 'a covenant falling to be complied with in relation to a particular part of the premises'. The effect of these subsections is as follows:

Section 28(2)   Covenants other than covenants to pay money

A covenant other than a covenant to pay money falls to be complied with in relation to a particular part of the premises if it 'in terms applies to that part of the premises' or 'in its practical application it can be attributed to that part of the premises (whether or not it can also be so attributed to other individual parts of those premises)'.

It cannot be said with optimism that this carries us much further forward.

Section 28(3)   Covenants to pay money

This clearly must mean covenants expressed as money payments. A covenant falls to be complied with in relation to a particular part if it 'in terms applies to that part' or the amount is determinable by reference:

>   (i)   to that part, or

(ii)   to anything failing to be done by or for a person as tenant or occupier of that part (if it is a tenant covenant), or

(iii)   to anything falling to be done by or for a person as landlord of that part (if it is a landlord covenant).

Section 10   Binding apportionments

Where, on an assignment (whether of the lease or of the reversion) of part of the assignor's holding under a lease, an agreement is made between the assignor and the assignee under s. 9 apportioning their liability then they can use s. 10 to make that agreement binding upon other persons.

The first stage is to serve a notice on the appropriate person. The form of notice is prescribed by the Lord Chancellor under s. 27(1). This is reproduced in appendix 3. It must be served either before or within four weeks of the assignment and this time limit cannot be extended.

The 'appropriate person' is defined by s. 10(4) by reference to the definition in s. 9(7). It is simply the landlord or landlords or tenant or tenants as the case may be of the entirety of the premises assigned by the assignor. An application may also be made (see s. 9(5)) for the apportionment to become binding on some person other than an appropriate person who is able to enforce the covenant. Such a person might be a management company which is able to enforce the landlord covenants.

A person (whether the appropriate person or some other person) may become bound by the apportionment:

(a)   By failing to serve a counter-notice within four weeks of service of the notice (s. 10(2)(a)). The counter-notice forms part of the notice served on the person who is to be bound (see appendix 3).

(b)   By a court declaration that the apportionment should be binding (s. 10(2)(b)).

An application is necessary if a counter-notice is served. It appears from the wording of s. 10(2)(b) that the application to the court must be made by each of the parties to the apportionment agreement. This will require an agreement between them about how they will conduct and share the costs of the application.

The Act requires the court which hears an application to decide whether it is 'reasonable for the apportionment to become binding'. No criteria for coming to the decision are laid down by the Act. However, the obvious question to ask is whether the assignor and the assignee are as good and reliable covenantors as each other in respect of this liability — or, more particularly, whether the assignee is as good and reliable a covenantor in respect of the liability from which the assignor is relieved.

(c) The appropriate person (or other person) served with a notice under these provisions may serve a notice consenting to the apportionment. This notice also forms part of the notice served on the person to be bound by the appointment. It is hard to see when this is likely to happen except as part of a bargain entered into by the various parties.

Section 11   Excluded assignments

Section 11 is a key provision to understanding the whole framework of the Act. There are a number of circumstances where a lease passes from one tenant to another without an act of the tenant. Amongst these are:

(a)   vesting on bankruptcy,*

(b)   vesting on dissolution of a company,*

(c)   revesting on repudiation of a gift,
      (the original tenant is liable as if there had never been a gift)

(d)   vesting on grant of probate,*

(e)   vesting on death of a tenant for life,*

(f)   vesting on grant of administration,*

(g)   a sale by a mortgagee,

(h)   a sale under a power,

(i)   vesting by order of court,

(j)   vesting on compulsory purchase.*

*Those asterisked are in fact excluded assignments and this is explained below.

The structure of the Act is that where the assignment is by the tenant the tenant's release from tenant covenants is intended to be effective from that assignment. Where the 'assignment' falls within s. 11 the release does not take effect until there is a further assignment which does not fall within s. 11.

The distinction between assignments by the tenant and assignments by operation of law is important. There is no definition of the term 'by operation of law' in the Act or in case law. However, it can be assumed that all cases where the tenancy passes to another other than by an act of some person are assignments by operation of law. Every case of transmission of a tenancy must fall into one of these two groups for the Act leaves no sensible scope for a third category except for assignments in breach of covenant of a tenancy (which fall within the class of excluded assignments as a special case).

As to the application of the term 'assignment' there is some further help given in old cases of which the clearest is *Baily* v *De Crespigny* (1869) LR 4 QB 180. Here, relying purportedly on *Spencer's Case* (1583) 5 Co Rep 16a, the court said (at p. 186), 'The word "assigns" is a term of well-known signification, comprehending all those who take either immediately or remotely from or under the assignor, whether by conveyance, devise, descent, or act of law'. Assuming that 'act of law' is equated with 'operation of law' this statement clearly makes room for the unwanted 'third category' in interpreting the 1995 Act.

Section 28 contains two very important provisions. First there is a definition of 'assignment' in s. 28(1):

. . . 'assignment' includes equitable assignment and in addition (subject to section 11) assignment in breach of a covenant of a tenancy or by operation of law.

Secondly there is an elaboration of this in s. 28(6):

For the purposes of this Act—

(a) any assignment (however effected) consisting in the transfer of the whole of the landlord's interest (as owner of the reversion) in any premises demised by a tenancy shall be treated as an assignment by the landlord of the reversion in those premises even if it is not effected by him; and

(b)   any assignment (however effected) consisting in the transfer of
the whole of the tenant's interest in any premises demised by a tenancy
shall be treated as an assignment by the tenant of those premises even if
it is not effected by him.

The case that at first appears anomalous is a sale by a mortgagee. This can
be used to illustrate how the Act operates. Where the sale is in exercise of
the statutory power of sale then ss. 88, 89 and 104 of the LPA 1925 give the
mortgagee power to vest the mortgagor's estate in the purchaser. The
conveyance is certainly not a case 'where a tenant assigns' (s. 5 of the 1995
Act). It is an act of the mortgagee. Nevertheless, to give the Act a consistent
framework this nagging doubt, as to the definition of excluded assignments
must be firmly discarded and a conveyance by a mortgagee viewed either as
an assignment by operation of law and hence an excluded assignment within
s. 11 or as a non-excluded assignment. Where an equitable mortgagee
conveys the legal estate the power to convey will arise from a power of
attorney. It is clear that ordinarily where a tenant assigns by an attorney the
assignment is not an excluded assignment. For consistency it must be that
assignments by act of the tenant and assignments by a person having a
power, statutory or otherwise, to convey the tenant's interest are not excluded
assignments. On this view a conveyance by a mortgagee is not an excluded
assignment and on such an assignment the mortgagor tenant is duly released.
The definition of assignment in s. 28(6) makes it perfectly clear that this is
in fact how the Act is intended to operate. An assignment is the transfer of
the landlord's or tenant's interest however effected 'even if it is not effected
by him'.

In the list given above the circumstances asterisked are excluded assignments. Those not asterisked are not. Transfer under an order of the court is
not an excluded assignment where it is to give effect to an obligation to
assign, e.g., to enforce a contract or a trust for sale. It is an excluded
assignment where the court is exercising a statutory power to redistribute
property, e.g., to vest property in a spouse on a divorce.

Assignments in breach of a covenant

An assignment in breach of covenant can still be effective as an assignment
(see, e.g., *Ideal Film Renting Co. Ltd* v *Nielsen* [1921] 1 Ch 575). The drafter
of the new Act decided that such an assignment will not release the tenant
from the tenant covenants. There is a breach of covenant if the assent of the
landlord is required but not requested (*Barrow* v *Isaacs and Son* [1981] 1

QB 417). It may often be difficult to tell if there has been an assignment in breach of a covenant restricting assignment. The issue in such a case will be resolved only if the reversioner brings an action for breach of the covenant.

Landlord's release

The position in respect of excluded assignments is the same, ceteris paribus, as for tenants. Thus, if L1 ceases to be landlord and the reversion vests by operation of law in L2 who sells the reversion to L3 then both L1 and L2 are entitled to apply for release. In practice L1 may not know about the assignment. However, the practical operation of this provision is unlikely to raise its head frequently. Most cases of assignment by operation of law will involve a landlord who (because of death or insolvency) has little interest in the future.

Section 11(4)

This provision will puzzle these who are faced with an assignment following an excluded assignment. Its effect is that assignments falling within s. 6(2) and (3) or s. 7(2) and (3) are excluded assignments. When a non-excluded assignment happens then s. 6 and s. 7 apply so that the landlord's release dates from the non-excluded assignment.

Section 11(5) and (6)

The effect of these tortuous provisions is as follows. Where there is an excluded assignment whether by the tenant or the landlord there cannot be an application under s. 9 for an agreed apportionment under s. 10. However, an agreed apportionment can be made effective at the time of the subsequent assignment.

Section 11(7)

Where there has been an excluded assignment, a subsequent assignment may be of only part of the premises. The provisions for release and apportionment will apply only to that part.

Section 12   Third-party covenants

There are many varieties of leasehold structure. Some are 'flat development schemes' designed for the commercial exploitation of blocks of flats. Some are schemes carefully constructed to provide a modus operandi for long-term management of the flats. In commercial schemes it is common to find a leasehold structure which has little connection with any rational approach to management as such. It may arise from some perceived fiscal advantage, the Byzantine workings of related companies or the happenstance of the market place.

The end result of such schemes is not uncommonly a position where a third party (a 'management company' typically) is responsible for carrying out maintenance, services or repairs. Because of the technicalities of landlord and tenant law such schemes are sometimes defective. The mischief is best seen from examples.

L is the freeholder of a block of flats developed and sold on long leases to 100 tenants. M is a management company which promises to carry out services etc. The type of problems which arise are:

  (a)   When a lease is assigned by a tenant, can the assignee be made to pay contributions to the management company?

  (b)   If the management company fails to carry out its obligations, is the landlord liable?

To address the position the scheme will often ensure that the relationship of landlord and tenant exists between each tenant and the management company. This may be done by granting the management company a concurrent lease or a head lease.

How does s. 12 fit into this very fragmented picture?

Section 12 applies to a covenant by a person 'other than the landlord or tenant' which is 'a covenant of a tenancy'. Where there are covenants such as the management company covenants described above, s. 12 applies in respect of any landlord and tenant situation where the person who has to perform an obligation is neither the landlord nor the tenant.

Once a particular covenant falls within s. 12, the third party is able to sue the assignee of the landlord and tenant as the case may be. An assignee of the landlord or tenant, as appropriate, is similarly also able to sue the third party.

To apply s. 12 it is necessary to find the person who is 'the landlord' and then the person who is 'the tenant'. Where there are a number of leasehold interests there will in respect of each tenant only be one person who is the landlord. That is the person who owns the reversion immediately expectant on the tenant's lease. Although this is perfectly clear at common law, s. 28(1) contains a definition to precisely that effect. In respect of different leasehold structures the relevance of s. 12 is as follows:

(a) If the management company satisfies the definition of landlord then s. 12 does not come into play so far as its covenants are concerned. This result may also follow because the management company has been granted a concurrent lease (see the comments on s. 15(1)).

(b) In a case where the management company satisfies the definition of landlord the freeholder (or the owner of any other reversionary interest) will not be the landlord. If there is an obligation to be performed by such a reversioner then s. 12 may be applied.

(c) If the management company or other person who is obliged to perform the landlord obligations has no interest in the property then s. 12 may apply.

(d) The same principles apply where the third party is liable to perform any obligation on behalf of the tenant.

Problems with section 12

Section 12 does not apply to guarantees or surety covenants (s. 12(1)(b)). Part of this provision may cause a problem in construction. Section 12(1)(b) provides that s. 12 does not apply where what is in question is 'financial liability referable to the performance or otherwise of a covenant in the tenancy by another party to it'. A not uncommon clause in a flat scheme is one to the following effect:

If the management company shall unreasonably fail to perform any of its obligations herewith the lessors on the request in writing of the lessee shall perform such obligation or obligations and any payment by the lessee in respect thereof shall be made to the lessors instead of the management company.

Such a clause will not fall within the exception for guarantee and surety covenants in cases where the lessor under the clause is the landlord within

s. 28. That is because in such a case s. 12 does not apply and instead the basic principles for the running of landlord and tenant covenants established by s. 3 apply.

There are cases where the lessor in such a case is not the landlord within s. 28. For example, L the freeholder has let a 999-year lease to T (a management company). L's obligation to make good T's failures to perform its obligations to the subtenants in possession will not fall within s. 12. There are two reasons for this. First the freeholder is not liable *as principal* as is required by s. 12(1)(a) but only as a surety or fall-back covenantor. Secondly the liability is in reality a guarantee of the performance by the management company.

Section 12 is expressed to apply only where the covenant is one 'to discharge any function with respect to all or any *of the demised premises*'. If there is a block of flats with a freeholder (F) and a management company (M) and 20 tenants (T1 to T20) then all that is demised to a tenant is a flat. What is a function in respect to the demised premises? For T20 on the ground floor it is hard to say how repairing the roof, or the lifts or the exterior can be a function in respect to the demised premises. However, to make any real sense of s. 12, it must apply to functions in relation to undemised common parts. The court could possibly reach this result by giving a wide meaning to the words 'with respect to' so as to include repair etc. of common parts related to the demised premises. This, though, would require a very strained interpretation of the words used.

Section 12(5)   Release of the landlord

On assigning a reversion, a landlord may wish to be released from obligations to a third party. If so the landlord must serve notice under s. 8(1) on the third party.

Section 13   Joint liability

Section 13(1) provides that where in consequence of the 1995 Act two or more persons are bound by a covenant then they are jointly and severally bound.

It appears clear from the rather odd wording of s. 28(4) that this provision does not deal with the case of persons who together are either the landlord or the tenant of a particular lease (see page 51).

Section 13(2) provides that a release of one of a number of persons jointly and severally bound by the same covenant does not release the others. This is subject to the provisions of s. 24(2) which deals with the effect of release of a tenant on a security or guarantee covenant.

Section 13 will apply to a tenant where there has been an excluded assignment. It will apply to landlords who have assigned their reversion but failed or decided not to obtain release from their obligations. It may also apply where there has been an assignment of part and there has been no apportionment of non-attributable covenants (see pages 19—20). The provisions as to liability must be carefully borne in mind when agreements for such release are considered.

Section 13(3) applies the Civil Liability (Contribution) Act 1978 to claims between persons jointly and severally liable on covenants as a result of the 1995 Act. It does this by defining such liability as 'damage' within s. 1 of the 1978 Act.

The Civil Liability (Contribution) Act 1978 is applied as if s. 7(2) of that Act were omitted (s. 13(3)(c) of the 1995 Act). The effect of this is that its provisions when applied under the 1995 Act can apply to breaches of obligation whenever they occurred. However, persons can become bound jointly and severally by virtue of the 1995 Act only after it comes into force.

Section 14 Abolition of indemnity covenants

The effect of s. 14 is to introduce two regimes for the future for indemnity covenants between tenants and assignee.

Old leases

Indemnity covenants between tenant and assignee continue to be implied as follows:

(a) LPA 1925, s. 77(1)(C). This implies a covenant on the assignment for valuable consideration of all the land in a lease. It does not apply to mortgages. The covenant (see appendix 2) is that the assignee will pay the rent, perform the covenants and indemnify the assignor. This covenant, unless varied by the parties, endures for the residue of the term or interest created by the lease. If there has been a legally apportioned rent in respect of part of the land in a lease then the covenants in s. 77(1)(C) are implied in the same way as if the apportioned rent was the original rent and the lease was solely of that land. A formal apportionment requires the concurrence of the lessor.

(b) LPA 1925, s. 77(1)(D). This implies a covenant similar to that in s. 77(1)(C) into an assignment for valuable consideration of part of the land in a lease. It applies where the rent has been informally apportioned whereas s. 77(1)(C) applies where the rent is apportioned with the consent of the lessor.

(c) Land Registration Act 1925, s. 24(1)(b) and (2). In relation to registered transfers of registered land, these sections imply covenants similar to those in the LPA 1925, s. 77(1)(C) and (D). Unlike the LPA 1925 provisions, s. 24 of the Land Registration Act 1925 applies to assignments which are not for valuable consideration.

New leases

In respect of new leases there is in general no need for the implication of covenants by the LPA 1925, s. 77, and the Land Registration Act 1925, s. 24(1)(b) and (2), and for new tenancies these provisions are abolished by s. 14 of the 1995 Act. This is because the assigning tenant ceases to be under any liability and, therefore, does not require an indemnity covenant. Where an assigning tenant enters into an authorised guarantee agreement (AGA) then the position between the assignor and the assignee is governed by the rules of law relating to guarantees (s. 16(8)). In particular the surety is entitled to stand in the shoes of the creditor and recover any indemnity paid from the tenant whose liability has been guaranteed. The rights of the guarantor arise by law out of the relationship between guarantor and debtor, and the guarantor need not wait until an indemnity is demanded or paid — it may at any time pay the creditor itself and recover the debt from the principal debtor (see, e.g., *Swire* v *Redman* (1876) 1 QBD 536 in which it was said that there is no known case of a guarantor ever exercising the right last mentioned to pay the creditor in advance of a demand!).

Section 15   Enforcement of covenants

The elusively phrased provision in s. 15(1)(a) enables persons who stand in the landlord's shoes to enforce landlord covenants. This applies to the grantee of an overriding or concurrent lease from a landlord. This is not an assignment by the landlord (s. 28(5)) — this is to prevent the landlord obtaining a release on such an event. However, the tenant of the overriding lease is not the reversioner within s. 15(6) but is the holder of the immediate reversion within s. 15(1)(a). This is different from the law applicable to old leases where the tenant of a concurrent or overriding lease is treated as an assignee of the reversion (LPA 1925, s. 149(5)). The definition of assignment in s. 28(5) makes s. 15(1) necessary if covenants of existing leases are to be enforced by or against such a grantee.

By virtue of s. 15(1)(b) covenants are also enforceable by a mortgagee in possession.

The tenant can enforce the landlord covenants against any person falling within s. 15(1)(a) or (b). This is the effect of s. 15(2).

Section 15(3) provides that the landlord covenants are enforceable by the tenant's mortgagee in possession. The tenant covenants and a right of re-entry in the tenancy are similarly enforceable against the tenant's mortgagee in possession (s. 15(4)).

Saving for personal covenants

The provisions of s. 15 do not make personal covenants enforceable against mortgagees and other third parties. This is because s. 15(5)(a) excepts from s. 15 'a covenant which (in whatever terms) is expressed to be personal to any person'. (Further comment on these words is given at page 7.)

Saving for registration

Section 15(5)(b) makes it clear that a covenant does not become enforceable against a person by virtue of s. 15 if it would otherwise be unenforceable because it was not registered under either the Land Charges Act 1972 or the Land Registration Act 1925. For example, a lease contains an obligation by a tenant which is registrable as a land charge such as an option in favour of the landlord. This should be registered against the tenants as a Class CIV land charge. If it is not then it is not binding upon a legal mortgagee (Land Charges Act 1972, s. 4(6)).

Section 16   Authorised guarantee agreements

The scheme of the 1995 Act is that on an assignment of a new tenancy the assignor is released. Section 16, however, permits the use of authorised guarantee agreements (AGAs) to provide some continuing liability of the former tenant.

If a new lease has been assigned by a former tenant then that tenant can be liable only under an AGA — unless the assignment was an excluded assignment (see page 22).

The requirements to be met to create a valid AGA are as follows:

(a) It must be an agreement under which the tenant guarantees the performance of the covenant by the assignee (s. 16(2)(a)).

(b) There must be a covenant in the lease preventing the assignment in question being entered into without the landlord's consent.

(c) The landlord's consent to the assignment must have been subject to a condition lawfully imposed which requires the tenant to enter into an AGA and the AGA must have been entered into pursuant to that condition. This means that landlords will seek to draft all new assignment provisions to include a condition that the tenant on assignment enters into an AGA. (See further page 58 and precedent at page 197.)

Section 16(5)   Terms forbidden in an AGA

An AGA must not impose on the tenant a guarantee which extends beyond the liability of the immediate assignee. Neither must it impose any guarantee in respect of performance by any person other than the assignee.

Any provision which purports to have the forbidden effect described is to that extent prevented from being an AGA. It can, thus, still be an effective AGA even though it contains ineffective terms.

Section 16(5)   Terms permitted in an AGA

Section 16(5) lists the matters which may be covered in an AGA. The former tenant may be made liable for any obligation of the assignee under the lease or made liable as a guarantor for such liability. It may also require the former tenant to enter into a new lease if the tenancy is disclaimed but such a new lease must not be for a longer term than the term assigned nor on more onerous terms.

Section 16(6)   AGAs following excluded assignment

Section 16(6) applies as follows. A lease to T1 may as a result of an excluded assignment (s. 11) become vested in T2. On a subsequent assignment T1 may be released under s. 11(2). If the assignor on that assignment enters into an AGA then T1 may be required also to enter into one.

Section 16(7)   AGAs following disclaimer or substitute Tenancy

A tenant may be required to enter into an AGA despite having already entered into one if the lease has been revested in the tenant following a disclaimer on behalf of the previous assignee.

Similarly a former tenant may be required to enter into an AGA on the assignment of a new tenancy which the former tenant has been required to take under a previous AGA. This would happen where T1 assigned to T2 with an AGA; T2 disclaimed and T1 was required to enter into a new tenancy. In this example when T1 assigns to T3 he may be required to enter into an AGA. T1's liability will only come to an end at last when T3 makes a non-excluded assignment to T4.

Section 17   Restriction on rent recovery

This extremely important provision applies both to new and old leases. It imposes a procedure for the recovery of money from former tenants and the guarantors of former tenants. It applies to new tenancies where the tenant is bound under an AGA (s. 16) and to an old or new tenancy in any case where a former tenant or its guarantor is still bound.

The section applies to any covenant 'under which a fixed charge is payable' (s. 17(1)). The expression 'fixed charge' is defined by s. 17(6). It includes rent or service charge payment. It does not matter that either of these is not in fact an unvarying sum under the tenancy agreement. Any obligation to pay rent, however the sum is determined, falls within s. 17. So far as service charge is concerned any service charge which falls within the definition in s. 18 of the Landlord and Tenant Act 1985 is included, with that definition widened to include service charges in all tenancies not just tenancies of dwellings.

The third category in the s. 17(6) definition of a fixed charge is as follows:

any amount payable under a tenant covenant providing for the payment of a liquidated sum in the event of a failure to comply with any such covenants.

A liquidated sum is defined clearly in *Halsbury's Laws of England*, 4th ed., vol. 9, para. 625, n. 8, as being

in the nature of a debt, i.e. a specific sum of money due and payable under or by virtue of a contract. Its amount must be ascertained or ascertainable as a mere matter of arithmetic.

The same definition is repeated in the *Supreme Court Practice 1995*, n. 6/2/4, which adds:

If the ascertainment of a sum of money, even though it be specified or named as a definite figure, requires investigation beyond mere calculation, then the sum is not a 'debt or liquidated demand', but constitutes 'damages'.

Both sources refer further to *Knight* v *Abbott* (1882) 10 QBD 11 but this case adds nothing of relevance. In the context of landlord and tenant law the distinction is between a fixed sum and a sum remaining to be assessed. If that fixed sum is a penalty and not a genuine pre-estimate of the damages it will not be recoverable in any event as normal contractual principles apply to damages in landlord and tenant cases (see further *Woodfall's Law of Landlord and Tenant*, para. 1–0724– et seq.).

In respect of any sum which is a fixed charge within s. 17 a strict procedure for recovery is provided.

The landlord must serve a notice within six months of the charge becoming due. The form of notice to be used is prescribed under s. 27(1) of the Act.

The notice must state that the charge is due and that the landlord intends to recover it from the former tenant or a guarantor (as the case may be).

Avoidance of section 17

Section 17 is Draconian. In the past landlords would commonly not look for reimbursement from a former tenant without some correspondence and negotiation and so on with the existing tenant. The six-month period will thus, very often have passed. However, the six-month period starts running only 'beginning with the date when the charge becomes due'. If in the original lease there is a provision for the tenant to pay rent then so far as the former tenant is concerned each instalment becomes due according to the term of the lease. The lease could, however, contain the following covenant:

> The tenant promises to pay the rent (etc.) except that a former tenant promises to pay the rent only when it is demanded.

A provision to the same effect can readily be included in an AGA so that the obligation to pay rent arises only when it is demanded. This advice works, of course, only if the words in s. 17(3) — 'six months beginning with the date when the charge becomes due' — mean 'become due against the former tenant' and not if they mean 'become due against the tenant in possession'. There is also the possibility of the drafting falling foul of the anti-avoidance provisions in s. 25 (see below).

Section 18   Variation of covenants

At common law there was some uncertainty about the effect on a former tenant or guarantor of a variation of covenants in a lease agreed to by an assignee and the landlord. As from 1 January 1996 such variations are governed by s. 18 of the 1995 Act.

Section 18(2)   Effect on the former tenant

The former tenant is not liable to pay any amount which is due to what is called a 'relevant variation'. This concept is defined in s. 18(3). It includes any variation which the landlord had an absolute right to refuse. It also includes variations falling within the tortuous provisions of s. 18(4)(b). This says that a variation is a relevant variation if the landlord had the right against a tenant to refuse a variation; the tenant has assigned and following the assignment the covenants have been altered so that the landlord no longer has the right to object to the variation in question.

The question whether a landlord has the right to refuse to object to a variation includes consideration of the effect of any legislation which gives the tenant the right to object to a variation (s. 18(5)).

Variations of covenants can fall within s. 18 whether they are by deed or otherwise (s. 18(7)). Even a variation which takes effect by way of estoppel may be included.

The effect of s. 18 is not very different from that under the common law as finally determined by *Friends Provident Life Office* v *British Railways Board* [1995] 48 EG 106.

The net effect of s. 18 is as follows:

(a)   An increase in the burden of the lease caused by operation of the original covenants will not release a former tenant. A good example is an increase in rent under a rent review clause. This is not a variation of the lease.

(b)   A variation which amounts to a surrender and regrant will release a former tenant. The only variations which have this effect are:

(i)   an express surrender and regrant;

(ii)   increase in the length of the lease; and

(iii)   an increase in the demised property.

(c)   In respect of any other variation the tenant's liability cannot be increased beyond that in the unvaried lease.

(d)   The rule in s. 18 cannot be altered by a term of the lease (see s. 25 (anti-avoidance provisions) discussed below).

Section 18(3)   Effect on the guarantor

Section 18(3) deals with the liability of a guarantor. It applies only if the guarantor is not otherwise wholly discharged by the variation. Accordingly the first step in this case is to consider whether a variation has discharged the guarantor. The modern law on this derives from *Holme* v *Brunskill* (1877) 3 QBD 495, in which Cotton LJ said, at pp. 505–6:

The true rule . . . is, that if there is any agreement between the principals with reference to the contract guaranteed, the surety ought to be consulted, and that if he has not consented to the alteration, although in cases where it is without inquiry evident that the alteration is unsubstantial, or that it cannot be otherwise than beneficial to the surety, the surety may not be discharged; yet, that if it is not self-evident that the alteration is unsubstantial, or one which cannot be prejudicial to the surety, the court, will not, in action against the surety, go into an inquiry as to the effect of the alteration . . . and that if [the surety] has not so consented he will be discharged.

There are three classes of variations which will not, at common law, discharge a surety and these are:

(a) Variations to which the surety has consented.

(b) Variations which are insubstantial.

(c) Variations which cannot prejudice the surety.

Clearly the operation of the common law rule leaves little scope for application of the new statutory provision. But, before teasing this out it is necessary to look at how the rule in *Holme* v *Brunskill* has been interpreted in case law.

(a) The surety is not discharged by a variation of the lease unless the variation has the effect of varying the terms of the guarantee. In *Metropolitan Properties Co. (Regis) Ltd* v *Bartholomew* [1995] 1 EGLR 65, Mitchell J said, at p. 67, that: '. . . a distinction exists between a variation of the earlier contractual terms and a variation of an obligation created under the terms of the earlier contract which variation itself encompassed those same terms'. The landlord had varied the tenant's assignment covenant by permitting shared occupation during the term but this did not alter the nature of the surety covenant which was to guarantee the tenant's obligations under the lease.

(b) It appears from *Holme* v *Brunskill* that the principle can apply to a surrender of part of the land in a lease in return for a reduced rent. In that case the lease was of a sheep farm in Cumbria which included a field which was surrendered and the rent reduced by £10 a year. This released a bondsman from his guarantee of the number of sheep to be returned at the end of the lease.

Giving time

There is a well-established rule that an agreement by a landlord to give a tenant time to pay an outstanding liability can release a surety. The principle on which this is based is explained with clarity in *Swire* v *Redman* (1876) 1

QBD 536. By agreeing to release the tenant for a period of time the landlord is said to prejudice the surety by interfering, in however small a way, with the surety's right to stand in the landlord's shoes and sue the tenant.

Because of this principle it is usual to provide in a surety covenant a proviso to the effect that:

> . . . any neglect or forbearance of the lessor in endeavouring to obtain payment of the rents hereby reserved when the same become payable or to enforce performance of the several covenants herein on the lessee's part contained and any time which may be given to the lessee by the lessor shall not release or exonerate or in any way affect the liability of the guarantor under this covenant.

This form of words was considered in *Selous Street Properties Ltd* v *Oronel Fabrics Ltd* [1984] EGD 360. A tenant had added toilets in breach of covenant but was given permission, by a licence to assign, to keep them there until the end of the lease. This forbearance came within the proviso quoted and the surety was not relieved by the landlord's forbearance.

The effect of s. 18(3) is that to the extent that a variation (by permitting the breach to continue) increases the surety's liability the surety is released from the guarantee even if there is a proviso like the one considered in *Selous Street Properties Ltd* v *Oronel Fabrics Ltd.*

In *West Horndon Industrial Park Ltd* v *Phoenix Timber Group plc* [1995] 1 EGLR 77 consideration was given to a similar clause but providing that the guarantee would subsist notwithstanding 'any other act or thing whereby but for this provision the Guarantor would have been released'. The variation which occurred was in a licence to assign which permitted the landlord to enter and make improvements which would have the potential of increasing the rent on a rent review. The court held the guarantor was released and the proviso was not intended to cover such a variation. The words applied only to the obligations in the original lease. If it was intended to cover additional burdens to be extracted from the tenant then this had to be done either expressly or by a much clearer implication.

A similar proviso was considered in *Howard de Walden Estate Ltd* v *Pasta Place Ltd* [1995] 1 EGLR 79. In a licence to assign, the tenant of a restaurant was permitted more tables and a more liberal sale of alcohol. This would on the face of it release the surety. This effect was not prevented by a proviso which said, '. . . any neglect or forbearance of the landlord in endeavour to obtain payment of the rents hereby reserved when the same become payable or to enforce performance of the . . . covenants and obligations on the part of the tenant herein or [in] any deed or documents supplemental hereto contained and any time which may be given whether to the tenant by the landlord or the landlord by the tenant shall not release or exonerate or in any way affect the liability of the surety under this covenant'. That proviso was aimed at situations where there was a breach by the tenant not where the lease was varied in its favour.

The proviso may be varied to provide that the surety is not affected by a surrender of part; or is not affected by any alteration of any term of the lease contained in a licence to assign or otherwise or in any other way which landlords in future feel advantageous. However, the effect of s. 18(3) is that where the surety is not discharged at common law by a variation (in these cases because in the surety covenant the surety has agreed not to be) the surety's liability cannot be increased by such a variation. This takes effect notwithstanding any provision to the contrary (s. 25 discussed further below).

Section 19   Overriding leases

The 1995 Act introduces a remedy for a former tenant who has been called upon by a landlord to pay outstanding rent owed by a subsequent assignee. Until now the former tenant has had to make this payment without any real prospect of being able to recover the rent. The former tenant would be entitled either to a statutory indemnity or to an indemnity under the principle exemplified by *Moule* v *Garrett* (1872) LR 7 Ex 101. The new provisions, which apply to both new and existing leases are introduced by s. 19 with ancillary provisions in s. 20.

A former tenant or a guarantor of a former tenant ('the claimant'), who has received a notice from the landlord under s. 17 and who has paid the amount required in full together with any interest, may, under s. 19, insist on being granted an 'overriding lease' by the landlord. The claimant will then become the superior landlord to the defaulting tenant and will have the right to take steps to recover the payment made under s. 17, e.g., by forfeiting the defaulting tenant's lease and either occupying the property personally or assigning the overriding lease. It is important to note that an overriding lease can be demanded only where a person has paid in full 'an amount which he has been duly required to pay in accordance with s. 17'. Thus, an overriding lease can be demanded only if the money has been paid pursuant to one of the s. 17 procedures.

A claim for an overriding lease must be made to the landlord either when the claimant pays the amount due under s. 17 or within 12 months of that payment. It must be made in writing and must specify the payment by which the claimant is claiming to be entitled to an overriding lease. There is no prescribed form of notice, so it can be in any form, for example, a letter will suffice. A precedent found in appendix 4.

The requirements of s. 23 of the Landlord and Tenant Act 1927 do not apply to service of the request. Under s. 19(10) of the 1995 Act the request may be sent to the landlord by post. It is recommended that a request should always be sent by recorded delivery so as to avoid a later dispute about whether or not it was sent to the landlord.

A claimant for an overriding lease must always consider when is the best time to apply bearing in mind that once an application has been made, the applicant will have to pay legal costs (including the landlord's costs: s. 19(6)) and, if the lease is completed, stamp duty and land registry fees. A claimant will usually not make a request immediately the current tenant has failed to pay the rent on one of the rent payment dates in the lease. It will be advisable to wait for a while to see whether there is any genuine prospect of the current tenant paying the rent. Having said that, there may well be situations where the claimant is aware early on that the current tenant has no prospect of paying and in such a situation the request can be made once the s. 17 notice has been received, and indeed in such a case the landlord may cooperate by serving a notice as early as possible in order to facilitate this action.

A landlord who receives a request for an overriding lease must grant and deliver it to the claimant within a reasonable time of receiving the request (s. 19(6)). There is no definition in the 1995 Act of what will or will not constitute a reasonable period of time.

On being granted an overriding lease the claimant must give the landlord an executed counterpart of it and is also liable to pay the landlord's reasonable costs involved in granting the overriding lease. These will include both solicitors' and surveyors' fees. It is advisable for the claimant to seek an estimate of these costs at the outset. Failure to comply with these requirements will mean that the claimant will be unable to exercise any of the rights which would otherwise be exercisable under the overriding lease, such as the right to forfeit the existing lease.

A landlord can avoid having to grant a claimant an overriding lease by determining the original lease, e.g., by forfeiture or re-entry. In this situation the landlord can retain the claimant's payment and take steps to relet the property (see s. 19(7)).

Section 19(9)   Abandonment of claim

There are two situations where a claimant is not entitled to an overriding lease. These are first where the landlord has already granted an overriding lease which is still in force and secondly where someone else has made a request for an overriding lease which has not been withdrawn or abandoned. The former situation does not in any way prevent there being more than one overriding lease in respect of a property at any one time (see s. 19(7)).

A claimant may withdraw or abandon a request for an overriding lease at any time before it is granted, but will be liable for the landlord's reasonable costs incurred to the time of withdrawal or abandonment. Withdrawal must be by written notice to the landlord but there is no prescribed form and a letter will suffice. (A precedent found in appendix 4.) A request will be abandoned if the claimant fails to comply with a written request from the landlord to take all or any of the remaining steps which must be taken by the claimant before the overriding lease can be granted. The request must specify a reasonable period in which the claimant must carry out these steps. Again there is no prescribed form of notice and a letter will suffice. If, by the time the period specified in the landlord's request has expired, the claimant has failed to carry out these steps, the request is regarded as abandoned. It is difficult to imagine that there will be many steps to be carried out by the claimant as once the overriding lease has been requested the only matters to be resolved are the form and content of that lease.

Section 19(8)   Competing claims to overriding lease

A situation may arise where two people, e.g., both a former tenant and a guarantor or two former tenants, claim an overriding lease on the same day. Only one of them will be able to have the overriding lease. In the former example the former tenant will be entitled to the overriding lease as s. 19(7)(a) treats his request as being made before the request by the guarantor even if the latter made his request earlier in the day than the tenant. In the second situation priority depends on whose liability started first, so that the claimant whose liability started the earliest is the one entitled to the overriding lease: the person whose debt arose first has the prior claim.

An overriding lease will be on the same terms as the existing lease subject to the following differences:

(a)   The term of the overriding lease will be for the remainder of the term of the existing lease plus three days, or, where the existing lease has only three days or less to run, the longest period being less than three days which will not displace the landlord's reversion (s. 19(2)).

(b)   Covenants in the existing lease which are expressed to be personal to the landlord and tenant are not to be included (s. 19(3)).

(c)   The claimant and the landlord may agree modifications to the terms of the lease (s. 19(2)(b)). There appear to be no restrictions to such modifications except that they must not amount to contracting out of the Act (see s. 25 below).

(d)   Where anything arising under a covenant in the existing lease is to be decided by reference to the start of that tenancy, e.g., the operation of a break clause or rent review, then the overriding lease must be framed in such a way that new clauses operate by reference to that date (s. 19(4)(a)).

(e)   Covenants which have been spent need not be included (s. 19(4)(b)).

(f)   The overriding lease must state that it is granted under s. 19.

(g)   It must state whether it is or is not a new tenancy for the purposes of s. 1: it will only be a new tenancy where the existing tenancy is a new tenancy.

Section 19(11) confirms that there is no limit on the number of overriding leases which can exist in respect of a property. In respect of an old lease this could arise, for example, where both the original tenant and the current tenant have been served with a s. 17 notice. In respect of a new lease it could arise, for example, where the original tenant or an assignee has been liable under an AGA.

Section 20   Provisions of overriding leases

Section 20(1) provides that it is only if the tenancy in respect of which there is a default is a new tenancy that the overriding lease is a new tenancy.

Section 20(2) provides that every overriding lease must state that it is granted under s. 19. It must state whether it is a new tenancy and comply with any relevant land registration rules. This statement must comply with the Land Registration (Overriding Leases) Rules 1995 (see appendix 3).

Section 20(3) contains the very important provision that failure by the landlord to provide an overriding lease in a reasonable time is a civil wrong in respect of which an action for damages will lie. A failure by the claimant to provide a counterpart will result in it not being allowed to exercise any rights under the lease.

Section 20(4) deals with the situation where a landlord who grants an overriding lease has mortgaged the property. In this situation the overriding lease is deemed to be authorised and is binding aginst the mortgagee. If the mortgagee has the landlord's title deeds then the landlord must within one month of the overriding lease being executed send the counterpart lease to the mortgagee. If the landlord fails to do so then the mortgage deed will apply as if the obligation to forward the lease were included in it and so the landlord will be in breach of the mortgage and liable to the consequent penalties. For completeness s. 20(7) confirms that 'mortgage' includes 'charge'.

Section 20(5) provides that the grant of an overriding lease is not a breach of any covenant against subletting or parting with possession. The provisions of ss. 16, 17 and 18 apply to overriding leases.

Section 20(6) provides that a claim to an overriding lease is registrable as an estate contract under the Land Charges Act 1972 or the Land Registration Act 1925. An overriding lease may itself require substantive registration under the Land Registration Act 1925 if it is a lease for 21 years or more. The right to an overriding lease is not an overriding interest under the Land Registration Act 1925, s. 70. Though the Act does not say so, if the consent of a superior landlord is required this must be overriden by the Act.

Section 21   Forfeiture or disclaimer of part

Section 21 applies only to new tenancies (s. 1(1)).

At common law forfeiture of part of the premises within a lease is possible (*Dumpor's Case* (1603) 4 Co Rep 119b). This principle was applied in *GMS Syndicate Ltd* v *Gary Elliot Ltd* [1982] Ch 1, in which Nourse J thought a forfeiture of part possible, at least 'where the two parts of the demised premises are physically separated one from the other and are capable of being distinctly let and enjoyed, and where the breaches complained of were committed on part of the property and on that part alone'.

The effect of s. 21(1) is that where it applies the landlord can forfeit only in relation to the part of the premises held by the tenant who has committed the breach of covenant. Three conditions have to apply. As a result of assignment the person in breach must be a tenant of only part of the premises. Secondly the lease being forfeited must contain a forfeiture clause. Thirdly the forfeiture must be '(apart from this subsection) exercisable in relation to that part and other land demised by the tenancy' (s. 21(1)(c)). If these conditions are satisfied then there can be a forfeiture only of the part of which the person in breach is tenant.

It is clearly possible to imagine circumstances where it is disadvantageous or even unfair to the landlord not to be able to forfeit in respect of the whole land contained in a tenancy. However, the rule in s. 21(1) does not admit of any flexibility. Its effect can be avoided in respect of forfeitures of new tenancies only by taking stricter control of assignments.

Section 21(2) deals with disclaimer of part. The powers to disclaim a lease in liquidation and bankruptcy are found in the Insolvency Act 1986. Sections 178 to 182 apply to liquidation and ss. 315 to 321 apply to bankruptcy.

In the past a lease had to be disclaimed as a whole or not at all. This was made clear in *Re Fussell, ex parte Allen* (1882) 20 ChD 341 explaining *Re Latham, ex parte Glegg* (1881) 19 ChD 7. (See also *MEPC plc* v *Scottish Amicable Life Assurance Society* (1993) 67 P & CR 314.)

Section 21(2) now provides that where, following assignment, there is a tenant of part only of the premises then the disclaimer can only be of that part. So far as this applies to bankruptcy it applies only if the trustee in bankruptcy is 'tenant of part only of the premises'. A tenancy held by a bankrupt vests in his or her trustee automatically as a result of the Insolvency Act 1986, s. 306.

Section 22   Landlord's consent to assignments

Section 22 introduces five new subsections to s. 19 of the Landlord and Tenant Act 1927.

These new provisions apply only to what is known as a 'qualifying lease'. This term is defined in a new s. 19(1E) of the Landlord and Tenant Act 1927. Qualifying leases are all new tenancies except any 'residential lease, namely a lease by which a building or part of a building is let wholly or mainly as a single private residence'. Section 19 does not in any case apply to leases of agricultural holdings (see s. 19(4)).

These amendments to s. 19 can be understood only in the context of the old law.

In the framework for a commercial lease in appendix 4, the assignment clause is clause 4.15. This sets out circumstances in which assignment is absolutely forbidden and then continues with the qualified covenant. The absolute part is 4.15(a). In so far as the covenant imposes an absolute ban on assignments etc. it does not fall within s. 19 at all. This proposition appears perfectly clear from the wording of s. 19 but was doubted (*obiter*) by Danckwerts LJ in *Property and Bloodstock Ltd* v *Emerton* [1968] Ch 94 at p. 119. However, the clearly correct view was stated by Browne LJ in *Bocardo SA* v *S & M Hotels Ltd* [1980] 1 WLR 17 who said:

> Since Parliament has not thought it necessary or desirable to prohibit or limit absolute covenants against assignment, I cannot discern any policy reason for invalidating a covenant which in effect prohibits assignment unless a condition precedent has been fulfilled.

The amendments to s. 19 are, thus, relevant only in cases where the landlord's consent to assign is required by the lease. In such cases the new provisions have the following effect:

Section 19(1A) allows an agreement between landlord and tenant to specify circumstances where the landlord may withhold consent or conditions subject to which consent may be granted. Where this is done, refusal of consent will not be unreasonable if the specified circumstances exist or the specified conditions are imposed. The Landlord and Tenant Act 1988, s. 1, takes effect subject to this change.

Section 19(1B) provides that an agreement under s. 19(1A) can be in the lease or in an extraneous agreement made before or after the lease is granted and at any time before application for the landlord's consent is made.

Section 19(1C) contains a very important qualification to s. 19(1A). That subsection does not apply where the conditions require a decision by the landlord or some other person unless one of two conditions is satisfied — either that decision must be made reasonably or the tenant must be given the unrestricted right to have that decision revised by an independent person whose decision is conclusive.

Section 19(1D) provides that s. 19(1)(b) does not apply to the assignment of a qualifying lease. (This means that if the assignment is a long building lease there is no proviso implied that no consent to assignment is required for any assignment before the last seven years.) This little change needs to be carefully watched because in respect of qualifying leases it puts building leases under the same regime as non-building leases.

Section 19(1E) gives the definition of qualifying lease already discussed. It also provides that assignment includes parting with possession on assignment.

The position can be summed up as follows:

(a)   No absolute covenant on assignment, however expressed, falls within s. 19(1).

(b)   Requirements for consent which are simply factual (requiring no determination by any person) cannot be challenged — but this adds virtually nothing to (a) in practical terms.

(c)   Requirements requiring a matter of judgment can now be made final by requiring a decision of an independent person. This is an important point and one that can be used to good effect in drafting. Doubtless the same result could have been achieved by careful drafting under the old law — but the terms of the new s. 19(1C) bring this to the fore.

Protracted delays and disputes in the area of consent to assignment are one of the negative aspects of landlord and tenant work. Inclusion of a speedy method for defining the acceptability (within the framework set by the lease) of a particular assignment should be very welcome.

The changes made to s. 19 apply only to assignments. They do not apply to consent for subletting or other dealings. This may well encourage more subletting.

Section 23   Breaches in respect of which new tenant is liable

Section 23 contains a number of points clarifying the nature of an assignee's position:

Section 23(1) provides expressly that an assignee does not as a result of the 1995 Act have any liability or rights in respect of any time before the assignment.

Section 23(2) provides that the liability and rights in respect of a period before the assignment *may* be assigned to the assignee. It may, for example, be desirable in a particular case for the assignee to take over liability for past arrears of rent as part of the deal which is struck at the time of the assignment.

Section 23(3) provides that where the benefit of a right of re-entry passes then it is exercisable in respect of a breach of covenant occurring before or after the assignment. So far as a breach of covenant before assignment is concerned it is not so exercisable if that breach has been waived or released so that it was not exercisable immediately before the assignment.

Section 24 Effect of releases

Where a person is released from a covenant by the operation of the 1995 Act, release does not affect any liability for breaches of covenant which occurred before the release (s. 24(1)).

Where a tenant is released by virtue of the 1995 Act, any guarantor of the tenant is also released *to the same extent*. In future guarantee covenants might sensibly be worded to make it clear that the guarantor's liability is limited to the period until the release from liability of the tenant who is guaranteed.

Section 24(3) provides that a person (either landlord or tenant) who assigns but is not released by virtue of the 1995 Act is similarly not released from liability in respect of any breach which occurred before the assignment.

If the effect of the 1995 Act is that a person loses the benefit of a covenant then the person does not lose any right arising in respect of a breach occurring before the assignment in question (s. 24(4)).

Section 25 Contracting out forbidden

Section 25 forbids contracting out from the 1995 Act. It does this by rendering any agreement void *to the extent* that it contravenes s. 25. This means that in drafting a lease a decision may be made to include provisions which contravene s. 25 but the only consequence of doing so is that the provision is void to the extent that it contravenes s. 25.

Section 25(1) Agreements affected

The agreements affected by s. 25 are:

(a) Agreements which 'have effect to exclude, modify or otherwise frustrate the operation of any provision of this Act' (s. 25(1)(a)).

(b) Agreements which provide for termination, surrender or the imposition of any penalty, disability or liability on the tenant in the event of the operation of the Act (s. 25(1)(b)) or in connection with or in consequence of the operation of the Act (s. 25(1)(c)).

An agreement may be affected by s. 25 whether or not it is contained in the tenancy agreement and whenever it is made (s. 25(4)).

Section 25(2)   Relationship between contracting out and assignment covenants

Covenants preventing assignment or requiring consent to assignment are not rendered void by s. 25. However, a covenant regulating assignment may fall foul of s. 25. It might link the giving of such consent to the operation of the provisions of the 1995 Act. The obvious way of doing this — by requiring the former tenant to guarantee the new tenant's obligations — is in any event permitted by the use of an AGA pursuant to s. 19. Section 25(3) provides expressly that s. 25 does not affect the operation of an AGA but that an agreement which falls foul of s. 16(4)(a) or (b) is void to that extent.

Section 26   Permitted releases

Section 26(1)(a) states that the 1995 Act does not prevent any party to a tenancy releasing a person from a landlord or tenant covenant.

A release may be personal to a particular tenant. This will not prevent the clause in question becoming binding on an assignee of that tenant (s. 3(4)).

The release of a tenant ordinarily releases any guarantee of that tenant's liability. This will apply to the liability of a former tenant under an AGA which complies with s. 16.

The release of a guarantee has no effect in itself on the liability of a tenant.

Landlord and Tenant Act 1985, section 3

Subsections (3A) and (3B) of s. 3 of the Landlord and Tenant 1985 provide that a former landlord's liability continues until the tenant is given notice of the assignment of the reversion and of the new landlord's name and address.

Section 26(2) of the 1995 Act provides that s. 3(3A) of the 1985 Act is unaffected by the new Act. Thus, a former landlord who is released under the provisions of the 1995 Act remains liable until the notice of assignment required by the 1985 Act is given.

Agreed apportionment

Section 26(1)(b) provides that nothing in the 1995 Act will prevent the parties agreeing to an apportionment of liability under a landlord or a tenant covenant.

Binding apportionments

Section 26(3) provides that once an apportionment has become binding under s. 10 it will not be affected by an order or decision made under any other Act 'which relates to apportionment'. There are a number of statutes with provisions for apportionment of liability in leases (e.g., the Landlord and Tenant Act 1927, s. 20). But s. 26(3) does not affect the operation of other statutes which do not deal directly with apportionment but permit variation of the position between persons whose liability was apportioned. For example, if the parties to the apportionment are husband and wife the power of the court to make a settlement (including varying the apportionment) under the Matrimonial Causes Act 1973, s. 24, is unaffected.

Section 27   Notices

Section 27 requires forms of notices for use under ss. 8, 10 and 17 to be prescribed by the Lord Chancellor. Those prescribed are set out in appendix 3.

It is made clear by s. 27(4) that notices 'substantially to the same effect' as the statutory notices can be effective. If a notice is not in the same form or substantially to the same effect then it is not an effective notice.

The forms of service permitted by the Landlord and Tenant Act 1927, s. 23 (which is set out in appendix 2) are permitted for service of notices under the 1995 Act (s. 27(5)).

Section 28   Interpretation

Section 28(1)   Definitions

The following expressions are defined by s. 28(1). The place where these definitions are discussed in the text is as shown in the list.

assignment (pp. 22 to 27)
authorised guarantee agreement (pp. 31 to 33)
collateral agreement (p. 9)
consent (pp. 44 to 46)
covenant (p. 7)
landlord covenant (pp. 7 to 9)
new tenancy (p. 6)
tenancy (p. 6)
tenant covenant (pp. 7 to 9)

*Section 28(2) and (3)   Covenant falling to be complied with in relation to
a particular part of the premises*

Subsections (2) and (3) of s. 28 amplify the concept of covenants falling to
be complied with in relation to a particular part of the premises. Section
28(2) deals with covenants other than covenants to pay money. Such a
covenant is attributable to part of the premises if either of two tests is
satisfied. First (s. 28(2)(a)) if it expressly applies to that part. Secondly
(s. 28(2)(b)) if in its practical application it can be attributed to that part —
even if it can also be attributed to other parts. Typical non-attributable
covenants would be covenants to repair the common parts not devised to any
tenant. It appears from the definition that a landlord covenant to repair, say,
the windows in demised premises is an attributable covenant because in its
practical application it applies to the windows in each part. A tenant covenant
to repair the plate-glass windows is similarly an attributable covenant.
However, a tenant covenant (given by a tenant of a house on a condominium
which shares an 18-hole golf course) to repair divots and pitch marks is a
non-attributable covenant where the course itself is not demised to any
tenant.

Section 28(3) is concerned with covenants to pay money which clearly must
mean covenants expressed as money payments. A covenant falls to be
complied with in relation to a particular part if it 'in terms applies to that
part' or (s. 28(3)(b)):

the amount is determinable by reference—

(i)   to that part, or

(ii)   to anything falling to be done by or for a person as tenant or
occupier of that part (if it is a tenant covenant), or

(iii)   to anything falling to be done by or for a person as landlord of that part (if it is a landlord covenant).

Thus, a covenant by a tenant of a shop to pay, as insurance rent, the cost of insuring the plate-glass windows in that shop is an attributable covenant. A share of the insurance rent of the whole building is a non-attributable covenant within this definition.

Section 28(4)   Joint liability

The provisions relating to joint and several liability contained in ss. 13, 24(2) and 28(4) are best considered together.

Section 28(4) is part of the interpretation provision in the Act. It provides that references in the Act to a landland or tenant are references to all the persons who jointly constitute the landlord or the tenant.

Section 13 provides that liability on a covenant is joint and several liability where it is the liability of more than one person.

Illustration of joint liability

(a)   A, B, C and D are partners in a firm of solicitors and are the tenants of Cross House. Where the Act refers to the tenant it refers to A, B, C and D together. Thus, the provisions of s. 13 referring to joint and several liability do not apply.

(b)   Cross House is leased to X who assigns half to A and half to B. So far as the covenants in the lease are concerned A and B may be liable on the same covenants in the lease as X and if so they are jointly and severally liable.

(c)   Cross House is leased by A to T1 who, having entered into an AGA, assigns to T2. The liability of T1 and T2 is joint and several by virtue of s. 13.

Section 28(5)   Assignment by landlord

The effect of s. 28(5) is that the 1995 Act applies where there is a transfer of the landlord's entire interest in all or part of premises but it does not apply where there is an assignment of part of the landlord's interest in all or part of premises such as by an equitable assignment or the grant of an overriding lease. In these cases there can be no release of the landlord.

Section 28(6)   Meaning of assignment

This is dealt with at pages 22 to 25.

Schedule 1, paragraph 1   Amendment of Trustee Act 1925, section 26

Where a tenant has died, his or her personal representative may be bound to enter an AGA in order to assign the lease. A new s. 26(1A) of the Trustee Act 1925 allows the personal representative to distribute the estate without appropriating any money for liability under this AGA and without any contingent personal liability as a result (s. 26(1A)(b)).

The result is as follows. Alf is tenant of Apple Stores. He dies and Betty becomes his sole executrix. As such she assigns to Curly and enters into an AGA which falls within s. 16. If Curly defaults and Betty has administered the estate she can when sued on the AGA plead *plene administravit*, which is a complete defence to liability.

Schedule 1, paragraph 2 Amendment of LPA 1925, section 77(2)

A new s. 77(2) of the LPA 1925 is substituted and the new subsection applies only to the conveyance of part of land subject to a rentcharge. The reference to a conveyance of part of land comprised in a lease is, thus, removed. This amendment applies only in relation to new tenancies (see s. 30(1)).

Schedule 1, paragraphs 3 and 4   Amendments of Landlord and Tenant Act 1954

Paragraph 3 makes an important amendment to s. 34 of the Landlord and Tenant Act 1954. That section provides for the fixing of a rent under part II of the 1954 Act. The amendment adds a new s. 34(4) to the effect that the provisions of the 1995 Act will be one of the factors taken into account in determining that rent. A renewal lease under the 1954 Act will be a new tenancy and thus subject to the new regime and this change is therefore perfectly appropriate.

Paragraph 4 amends s. 35 of the 1954 Act. It provides that in considering the terms of a new lease under that Act the court should take into account the 1995 Act.

3

The 1995 Act in Practice

Rent arrears

Arrears due on or after 1 January 1996

The provisions in the 1995 Act governing the landlord's right to recover arrears from a former tenant or a former tenant's guarantor are found in s. 17 and apply to new tenancies as well old tenancies. Section 17 does not apply to all sums which may be in arrears under a lease, only to those which are fixed charges. These are:

(a)   rent, which will include anything reserved as rent, such as insurance premiums,

(b)   service charge, and

(c)   any amount payable by a tenant as liquidated damages in respect of a breach of covenant.

It should be noted that (c) above will not cover unliquidated damages for breach of covenant, e.g., for breach of the alienation covenant.

'Service charge' is defined in the Landlord and Tenant Act 1985, s. 18, and covers any sum which is payable, either directly or indirectly, for services, repairs, maintenance or insurance or the landlord's costs of management. The whole or part of this sum may vary according to the relevant costs, which are the costs, real or estimated, which are incurred by or on behalf of a landlord in connection with the matters for which the service charge is payable.

The basic rule is that a landlord who wishes to recover arrears from a former tenant or a former tenant's guarantor must first serve a notice on the person from whom recovery is sought. The notice must be served within six months of the date on which the fixed charge being claimed fell due. If the notice is not served within this period the right of recovery is lost.

The form of notice which must be used is prescribed (see appendix 3) and states that:

(a)   the fixed charge is due, and

(b)   the landlord intends to recover the charge together with interest, if this is payable under the terms of the lease.

Once a notice has been served within the six-month period there is no requirement that proceedings be brought within a certain time though obviously they must be brought within the limitation period.

The persons on whom a s. 17 notice can be served are:

(a)   in the case of a new tenancy, the former tenant who has entered into an AGA and

(b)   in the case of an old tenancy, any former tenant who is liable on the covenants in the lease to pay a fixed charge, i.e., the original tenant and any intermediate tenants who have agreed to be liable after they have assigned, and their guarantors

(c)   in the case of a new tenancy any former tenant or guarantor who has not been released, i.e., because there is an excluded assignment.

Advising a landlord

The effect of s. 17 is that landlords will now have to be more proactive in the management of their properties. Landlords and their managing agents should be advised that they must review their procedures for recovering arrears from tenants so that the need for service of notices under s. 17 is automatically brought to their attention so that whenever arrears fall due for which former tenants and guarantors may be liable, s. 17 notices are sent to them. Before such notices are served, consideration should be given to whether the landlord will actually want someone to have the right to an overriding lease (see p. 39) or whether the landlord should forfeit the lease instead. Suppose that the current rent under a lease is £35,000 per annum and that the current market rent is £40,000 per annum. There are several prospective new tenants. In this situation it would be better for the landlord to forfeit the lease so that a new lease can be granted at the higher rent, rather than serving a s. 17 notice and having to grant an overriding lease at the existing rent and wait until the next rent review for an increase in the rent.

There may be other problems for a landlord who has to grant an overriding lease. For example, the overriding tenant may become insolvent and surrender the lease. The landlord may even decide that it is undesirable to have that person as a tenant again.

A solicitor or managing agent who does not advise a client landlord of these choices may be liable in negligence.

When a landlord has decided to serve a s. 17 notice it will be prudent to ensure that it is served as soon as possible after the sums in question have fallen into arrears so that no time is lost in recovering them. In any event the notice must be served within the six-month period. If it is not then the agent may be liable in negligence for failure to comply with the time limits.

Where a landlord has a team of professional advisors, for example a solicitor *and* a surveyor/managing agent, it must agree whose responsibility it will be for serving a s. 17 notice. If such an agreement is not made then there could be a danger that a notice is not served within the six-month period.

Advising a former tenant or a guarantor

A former tenant or a guarantor who receives a notice under s. 17 should be advised to contact the current tenant to find out whether the arrears have been or are going to be paid. There would be little point in the former tenant or guarantor paying them only to find out that the current tenant has just paid them. The recipient of a s. 17 notice must also be advised of the liability to pay the arrears should the current tenant fail to pay them. Advice should also be given on the right to request an overriding lease from the landlord and the procedures and time limits involved.

Increase in the arrears

Where a landlord has served a s. 17 notice and the amount of the fixed charge subsequently increases, a second notice must be served claiming the increased amount. This does not apply where the landlord is just claiming an increase in interest.

The form of this second notice is also prescribed (see appendix 3).

The increase to which the notice relates must be provided for in the lease and, for example, would be where the landlord is recovering a service charge payment and at the end of the relevant accounting period there is a balancing payment to be made.

There are two further requirements which must be satisfied before the second notice can be served and these are that:

   (a)   the original s. 17 notice told the former tenant or guarantor that the amount claimed would be subsequently revised, and

   (b)   the second s. 17 notice was served within three months of the revision.

The new notice must set out the new sum which is due together with any calculation of interest.

Arrears due before 1 January 1996

Any fixed charge which has become due before 1 January 1996 for which no recovery proceedings have been brought against a former tenant are treated under s. 17(5) as becoming due on 1 January 1996.

This means that a landlord owed arrears who did nothing about them before 1 January 1996 has six months (i.e., until 30 June 1996) to serve a s. 17 notice on the former tenant.

Section 17(5) disapplies s. 17(2) and (3) only if proceedings have been brought against a former tenant before 1 January 1996. This means presumably that if proceedings have been brought before that date against a guarantor but not the former tenant then the landlord must still serve a s. 17 notice against the former tenant before 30 June 1996, although the fact that proceedings were not brought against the former tenant would indicate that it was thought that recovery from that source would be unlikely. Even so serving a s. 17 notice may be prudent to cover the situation where the former tenant subsequently comes into money and is able to pay.

Liability of a former tenant or guarantor to pay an increase in rent due to a variation in the lease

Variations made on or after 1 Janury 1996

Under s. 18, where a lease has been varied on or after 1 January 1996, a former tenant will not be liable for any increase in the rent which is due to the variation, provided that the landlord had absolute discretion in deciding whether or not to agree to the variation. This can be best illustrated by an example.

Suppose a lease contains covenants by the tenant as follows:

(a)   Not to use the premises otherwise than as a betting shop or for such other use as may be approved in writing by the landlord, such consent not to be unreasonably withheld.

(b)   Not to sublet the whole or part of the premises.

After the lease has been assigned by the original tenant, and on or after 1 January 1996, the landlord agrees to change the first of these covenants to allow the premises to be used for any use within Classes A1 and A2 of the Town and Country Planning (Use Classes) Order 1987 and also agrees to vary the lease to allow subletting of part subject to consent. The effect of both these changes will be to increase the rent payable on a subsequent review. Alternatively it may be agreed that the tenant will pay a higher rent in return for the variations.

If the current tenant then fails to pay the new rent, the original tenant will only be liable to pay the rent which would have been due had the leases still contained a bar on subletting part of the property. The increase due to the variation in the user covenant will be payable by the original tenant as the landlord did not have absolute discretion in deciding whether to agree to this change.

Another example of a situation where a landlord does not have absolute discretion is where the change is allowed under statute, for example, where the tenant makes improvements under the Landlord and Tenant Act 1927, s. 3.

Variations made before 1 January 1996

Variations made to a lease before 1 January 1996 will not be subject to the 1995 Act but any subsequent variations made after the Act has come into force will be subject to the new law as discussed above.

Assignments

Assignment by the tenant

Existing leases   Leases entered into before 1 January 1996 remain subject to the rules of privity and so an original tenant will be liable under the tenant's covenants throughout the term of the lease even after assigning the lease unless release from this liability can be negotiated with the landlord. There will be few situations where a landlord will agree to abandon such a valuable covenant.

A tenant who does obtain a release will want it to be a full release from all liabilities under the covenant.

From a tenant's point of view, a covenant in the lease whereby the landlord agrees to take reasonable care to make sure that future assignees are financially sound and that the landlord must pursue the current tenant and guarantor, if any, before resorting to the original tenant are advisable. The Court of Appeal in *Norwich Union Life Insurance Society* v *Low Profile Fashions Ltd* [1992] 1 EGLR 86 refused to imply such terms into a lease and so they must be expressly included. For further discussion of this point see Murray Ross, *Drafting and Negotiating Commercial Leases*, 4th ed. (London: Butterworths, (1994), p. 59.

A tenant should always take an indemnity covenant from the assignee where one is not implied by statute (LPA 1925, s. 77 and sch. 2, parts IX and X; Land Registration Act 1925, s. 24).

Unlike an original tenant, an assignee is liable on the covenants only while holding the lease. An assignee who makes a further assignment is not liable for breaches by later assignees at common law. However, usually, a licence to assign makes the assignee liable for the remainder of the term of the lease even after a further assignment. This has the effect of making the assignee jointly liable with the original tenant until the end of the term. If this is done every time the lease is assigned then the landlord can pursue every person in whom the lease has been vested.

New leases   A tenant under a new tenancy will be automatically released from liability under the lease covenants on assigning the lease (see the 1995 Act, s. 5). However, a tenant may be required to enter into an AGA if this is provided for in the lease. This will make the original tenant liable under the covenants whilst the lease is vested in the assignee but this liability will come to an end when the assignee subsequently assigns the lease to another person. Hence there is no need in the lease for any covenants on the part of the landlord along the lines discussed above.

Section 30(2) and sch. 2 repeal the statutory implied covenants contained in the LPA 1925, sch. 2, parts IX and X. These were that, on the assignment for valuable consideration:

(a)   of the whole of the property, the assignee and his successors will pay the rent and comply with the covenants in the lease and indemnify the assignor, or

(b)   of part of the property:

(i)   the assignee and his successors in title will pay the apportioned rent, comply with the covenants in the lease which relate to the part of the property assigned and indemnify the assignor, and

(ii)   the assignor and his successors in title will pay the balance of the rent, comply with the covenants in the lease relating to the retained property and indemnify the assignee.

Further, in the case of the assignment of a registered lease, the 1995 Act repeals the Land Registration Act 1925, s. 24(1)(b) and (2). These imply similar covenants to those mentioned above.

Assignment of the reversion

Existing leases   An original or subsequent landlord will remain bound by the landlord covenants after assigning the reversion (see LPA 1925, s. 141).

New leases   An original landlord may be released from the landlord covenants on assigning the reversion provided the procedure contained in s. 8 of the 1995 Act is followed and the assignment is not an excluded assignment under s. 11. Unlike the release of the tenant, this release does not happen automatically but only after the landlord has served notice on the tenant. This is because a tenant has no way of making sure that an assignee of the reversion is financially sound.

The procedure which a landlord has to follow is that a notice must be served on the tenant. This notice must be in the prescribed form of which there are four, one each dealing with release on the assignment of the whole and part respectively and two for which a former landlord makes a request (see appendix 3) and must:

(a)   inform the tenant that either the assignment has taken place, or it is proposed to assign the reversion,

(b)   request that the landlord be released,

(c)   explain the significance of the notice and the options open to the tenant,

(d)   state that any objections to the proposed release must be made by written notice served on the landlord within four weeks of the day on which the notice is served, and

(e)   give an address in England and Wales to which objections may be sent.

Interestingly, the notice does not tell the tenant anything about the assignee. It appears that in order to find out who the assignee is, the tenant will have to object to the release and request more information from the assignor. Once he has this information and is satisfied with it, the tenant can then withdraw his objection.

The landlord must serve the notice on the tenant either before or within four weeks of the date of the assignment. This time limit is strict and there is nothing in the Act to allow it to be extended by agreement.

Having received the notice the tenant can either:

(a)   do nothing, in which case, once four weeks have elapsed from the date of service of the notice on the tenant, the landlord is released from the landlord covenants, or

(b)   serve a notice objecting. There is a prescribed form for this notice (see Appendix 3). A notice of objection must be served within four weeks of the landlord's notice being served. Again this is a strict time limit and cannot be extended.

If the tenant objects then the landlord could decide not to take it any further and so will remain bound by the covenants. Alternatively, the landlord could apply to the county court for a declaration that it would be reasonable to be given a release.

After having served notice of objection, the tenant may be content for the landlord to be released. If that is so the tenant can serve a written notice on the landlord withdrawing the notice of objection. There is no prescribed form and a letter will suffice. Presumably, if the landlord has made an application to the county court then it will be necessary to withdraw that application and the landlord may be able to insist on the tenant paying the wasted costs.

The landlord will be released as from the date of the assignment of the reversion (s. 6(2)(b)).

A landlord who is not released on assigning the reversion will have a further opportunity under s. 7 to apply to the tenant for a release every time there is a further assignment of the reversion. The procedure is the same as that discussed above. However, there may well be a problem in that the former landlord may not be aware of subsequent assignments of the reversion. A landlord should deal with this problem by taking a covenant from the assignee whereby the assignee will inform the original landlord when proposing to assign the reversion again. This will then allow the former landlord to serve a notice seeking release if desired.

Where a landlord is released on the assignment of the reversion the assignee's solicitor should consider amending the Standard Conditions of Sale, 3rd ed., so that Standard Condition 4.5.4 does not apply. Statute does not imply an indemnity covenant on the assignment of the landlord's reversion and so Standard Condition 4.5.4 provides for the buyer to covenant in the purchase deed to indemnify the seller against future liability under the covenants in the lease and, if the seller requires, to execute a duplicate transfer. If the landlord has been released then there is no need for the assignee to enter into such a covenant. This amendment should be made by including a special condition to the effect that Standard Condition 4.5.4 does not apply. However, if the landlord has not been released at the time of the assignment then the landlord will want an indemnity from the buyer and will therefore resist the exclusion of Standard Condition 4.5.4. In this case it may be prudent for the buyer's solicitor to require that any indemnity given by the buyer will last only until the seller is released in the future.

The landlord's release is also discussed on pp. 16 to 19.

Drafting alienation covenants

Absolute covenants

The 1995 Act makes no alteration to the position regarding absolute covenants.

Qualified covenants

The amendments which the 1995 Act makes to the law regarding qualified covenants and the Landlord and Tenant Act 1927, s. 19(1)(a), were said by the promoter of the Bill in the House of Lords, the Earl of Courtown, to represent the backbone of the compromise reached between the British Property Federation and the British Retail Consortium which allowed the Bill to be fully supported. In return for the loss of privity of contract, landlords have been given the right to lay down in advance the conditions in which consent to an assignment will be given. The provisions do not go so far as to allow a landlord complete control and if this is required a landlord can still impose an absolute covenant but this must be balanced against the lower rent which can be obtained from a tenant both initially and on review.

The intention of the new provisions is to allow the parties to set down in advance what the conditions will be for an assignment without being concerned that such conditions will be unreasonable. What is not possible is for the parties to agree that s. 19(1)(a) will not apply at all.

The new provisions are contained in s. 22 of the 1995 Act which amends s. 19 of the 1927 Act by inserting five new subsections after subsection (1).

These new provisions:

(a)   only apply in relation to the landlord's consent to an assignment of the lease and they do not affect consent in relation to anything else, e.g., underletting, charging etc.;

(b)   apply only if the tenancy is a new tenancy as defined in s. 1 of the 1995 Act;

(c)   do not apply to either agricultural tenancies, which have their own regime, or to residential tenancies; and

(d)   apply where a tenant parts with possession of the premises by way of assignment.

The main provisions are contained in the new s. 19(1A) of the 1927 Act. This allows a landlord and tenant to agree in advance either:

(a)   the circumstances in which the landlord may withhold consent to an assignment; or

(b)   any conditions subject to which consent will be given.

Where such an agreement has been entered into, it will not then be unreasonable for the landlord to withhold consent on the ground that any of the specified circumstances exist, or to give consent subject to the specified conditions.

If the tenant meets all the conditions which are specified in an agreement and the landlord still refuses to give consent, the landlord will have to prove that the final refusal is not unreasonable.

In any event a landlord will still be subject to the duties imposed under the Landlord and Tenant Act 1988.

The agreement between the parties may either be contained in the lease itself or in a separate document. An agreement in a separate document can be entered into at any time before the tenant applies to the landlord for consent to assign (s. 19(1B)). Normally the agreement will be contained in the lease but it may be appropriate to have it in a separate document where, for example, the agreement is personal to the particular tenant and will not be passed on to an assignee, or where it has been prepared in order to reflect a change in market conditions since the lease was granted.

The drafter of a lease will always have to consider whether restrictions need to be placed on the tenant's right to assign the lease, and instructions will need to be taken from the landlord on this point. The restrictions should form part of the initial negotiations between the parties. It is envisaged that there will not be one standard form of restriction which will be used but rather each lease will have specially drafted restrictions to suit the terms of the lease, the parties, the nature of the property which is being let etc. It must always be borne in mind that whatever restrictions are included there will be a consequential effect on any rent review provisions in the lease and these may need modifying accordingly (see page 73).

At the end of the day it will always be a matter for the parties to agree on the conditions and much will depend on their relative bargaining strengths.

The conditions which are permitted can be divided into two types. The first are conditions which are absolute in that if they are not satisfied consent will not be given. These will relate to the type of assignee which the landlord is prepared to accept, the time of assignment or the terms of the lease after assignment or of the assignment itself. As they will be known in advance a tenant will know that if the proposed assignee does not fulfil these requirements then there is little point in asking the landlord for consent as it will be refused. Examples of such conditions will include conditions that:

(a)   the assignor must enter into an AGA (this is likely to be the most popular condition);

(b)   the assignee must be supported by a rent deposit for a specified amount;

(c)   the assignee's most recent accounts must show net profits before taxation equivalent to a specified multiplier of the rent, e.g., three times the rent, and such accounts must be audited;

(d)   the assignee must not carry on a specified business or one which directly competes with that of the landlord or another specified person or company, such as another tenant in the centre or development;

(e)   where the assignee is a limited company, personal guarantees must be given by at least two directors;

(f)   all the tenant's covenants in the lease have been complied with; and

(g)   any outstanding rent review has been completed.

If the landlord subsequently refuses consent on an absolute ground then consent cannot be regarded as having been withheld unreasonably and that is the end of the matter.

Examples of restrictions which may be included in an alienation covenant are given in appendix 4.

One effect of the 1995 Act may be to reduce inter-company transfers. This is because the assignor company will be automatically released unless the landlord requires it to enter into an AGA, which may be of little value in the case of a subsidiary company, and/or requires the parent company to stand as guarantor. It has been suggested that a lease may provide that a landlord may withhold consent unless the assignee is a company within the same group of companies (T.M. Aldridge, *Privity of Contract: Landlord and Tenant (Covenants) Act 1995* (FT Law & Tax, 1995)). It is submitted that such a clause would not be in the interests of the landlord because of the automatic tenant release unless it is also provided that some form of guarantee is given.

The second type of condition is the discretionary condition, in other words the condition is dependent on the exercise of the landlord's discretion. Examples of such conditions would be where:

(a)   the assignee must in the landlord's opinion be of equal financial standing to the tenant, or

(b)   the assignee must not in the landlord's opinion be in competition with the landlord's business or that of a specified person or company.

See appendix 4 for examples of these.

In these cases the landlord has to exercise a discretion. Under the terms of the agreement this discretion must be exercised reasonably, or the tenant must be given an unrestricted right to have the landlord's determination reviewed by an independent person. In the absence of either of these the effect is that the landlord has to exercise the discretion reasonably within the old law (see chapter 4). The identity of the independent reviewer must be ascertainable by reference to the agreement which, as has been seen, can either be in the lease or in a separate document. The tenant's right will not be implied into the covenant and must be specifically mentioned otherwise the covenant will be subject to s. 19(1)(a) and the landlord will have to prove that the refusal of consent was reasonable. It must be expressed that an independent determination is conclusive of the matter in question.

Where the matter can be reviewed by an independent third party the agreement must provide for that person's identity to be ascertainable by reference to the agreement. This will include provisions which provide for an independent person to be appointed by a stated third party such as the President of the Royal Institute of Chartered Surveyors.

An example of each type of discretionary condition is given in appendix 4. These can readily be amended so, for example, the condition which has been provided as requiring the landlord to exercise discretion reasonably can be changed into one without that requirement and for the matter to be referred to an independent third party if the tenant disagrees with the landlord's decision.

Overriding leases

Under s. 19 of the 1995 Act a former tenant or guarantor who has been called upon under s. 17 by a landlord to pay outstanding rent owed by a subsequent assignee can apply to the landlord for the grant of an overriding lease. The former tenant or guarantor will then become the superior landlord to the defaulting tenant and will have the right to take steps to recover money paid to the head landlord, e.g., by forfeiting the defaulting tenant's lease and either occupying the property personally or assigning the overriding lease.

Making a request for an overriding lease

A request for an overriding lease must be made to the landlord either when the claimant pays the amount due under s. 17 or within 12 months of that payment.

The request must be made in writing and must specify the payment by which the claimant is claiming to be entitled to an overriding lease. There is no prescribed form of notice and so a request which is made by letter will suffice (see appendix 4 for an example of a notice of claim).

Once the request has been made it should be registered either as a C(iv) land charge in the case of unregistered land, or as a notice or caution where the land is registered. If this is not done it will not bind a purchaser of the reversion.

Service of the request

The requirements as to service of notices contained in the Landlord and Tenant Act 1927, s. 23, do not apply to service of a request for an overriding lease so, for example, it cannot be served by leaving it at the landlord's last known place of abode in England or Wales. There are, however, provisions as to service in s. 19(10) of the 1995 Act. These provide that the request may be sent to the landlord by post. It is recommended that a request should always be sent by recorded delivery so that proof is obtained. This will then avoid the possibility of a dispute arising about whether or not a request was sent to the landlord.

When should a request be made?

A claimant for an overriding lease must consider when the best time would be to apply for the overriding lease. It must be borne in mind that once an application has been made, both the applicant's and the landlord's costs will have to be paid by the applicant and, if the lease is completed, stamp duty and, possibly, land registry fees if the lease is registrable.

It is not envisaged that a claimant will make a request immediately after paying the amount due to the landlord. It may be advisable to wait for a while to see whether there is any genuine prospect of the current tenant making payment. Having said that, there will be occasions where the claimant is aware early on that the current tenant has no prospect of paying and in such a situation the request can be made once the s. 17 notice has been received, and indeed in such a case the landlord may cooperate by serving a notice as early as possible in order to facilitate this action.

Action by a landlord who receives a request

A landlord who receives a request for an overriding lease must grant and deliver to the claimant an overriding lease within a reasonable time of receiving the request (s. 19(6)). There is no definition in the 1995 Act of what will or will not constitute a reasonable period of time. If the landlord does not grant the overriding lease within a reasonable time the claimant may bring a civil action in tort for breach of statutory duty.

A landlord can avoid having to grant a claimant an overriding lease by determining the original lease, e.g., by forfeiture or re-entry. In this situation the landlord can retain the claimant's payment and take steps to relet the property (see s. 19(7)).

Withdrawal or abandonment of a request

A claimant may withdraw or abandon a request for an overriding lease at any time before it is granted, but will be liable for the landlord's reasonable costs incurred to the time of withdrawal or abandonment. Withdrawal must be by written notice to the landlord but there is no prescribed form and a letter will suffice (see appendix 4).

A request will be abandoned if the claimant fails to comply with a written request from the landlord to take all or any of the remaining steps which must be taken by the claimant before the overriding lease can be granted. The request must specify a reasonable period in which the claimant must carry out these steps. Again there is no prescribed form of notice and a letter will suffice. If, by the time the period specified in the landlord's request has expired, the claimant has failed to carry out these steps, the request is regarded as abandoned. It is difficult to imagine that there will be many steps to be carried out by the claimant as once the overriding lease has been requested the only matters to be resolved are the form and content of that lease.

Competing claims for an overriding lease

A situation may arise where two people, e.g., both a former tenant and a
guarantor or two former tenants, claim an overriding lease on the same day.
Only one of them will be able to have the overriding lease. In the former
example the former tenant will be entitled to the overriding lease as
s. 19(7)(a) treats his request as being made before the request by the
guarantor even if the latter made his request earlier in the day than the tenant.
In the second situation priority depends on whose liability started first, so
that the claimant whose liability started the earliest (that is, the one whose
debt is the oldest) is the one entitled to the overriding lease. For example, if
L grants a lease to T, who then assigns to A1 who later assigns to A2 and
A2 then defaults, and both T and A1 claim overriding lease on the same day,
T's liability has arisen before A1's and so T will be entitled to the overriding
lease.

Drafting the overriding lease

An overriding lease will be on the same terms as the existing lease subject
to differences set out on pp. 42 to 44. An example of an overriding lease is
found in appendix 4.

It appears from s. 19(2)(b) that the claimant and the landlord may agree
modifications to the existing lease and then include these in the overriding
lease. The 1995 Act goes no further on this point and so presumably the
parties could agree to include covenants, including personal covenants, in the
overriding lease which were not contained in the original lease or they could
agree that covenants in the existing lease are not to be included in the
overriding lease.

An overriding lease could set out in full all the terms of the existing lease or
alternatively could just incorporate these by reference (see page appendix 4).

Payment of costs

A claimant who is granted an overriding lease is liable to pay the landlord's
reasonable costs involved in granting the overriding lease. These will include
both solicitors' and surveyors' fees. It is advisable for the claimant to seek
an estimate of these costs at the outset. There is no mention of whether the
claimant is responsible for any disbursements incurred. Failure to comply
with these requirements will mean that the claimant will be unable to

exercise any of the rights which would otherwise be exercisable under the overriding lease, such as the right to forfeit the existing lease.

Situation where a section 17 notice is served on more than one former tenant

The 1995 Act does not specifically deal with the situation where a landlord is able to serve a s. 17 notice on more than one former tenant, e.g., where the former tenant comprises two or more joint tenants. Imagine a situation where the former tenant was a partnership and the lease was held in the names of several partners. When the lease was assigned the former partners entered into an AGA. The assignee has now defaulted and the landlord wishes to serve a s. 17 notice. Presumably the landlord has several options:

(a)   one notice could be served addressed to all of the partners, or

(b)   notices could be served on each of the partners individually.

The question is who can then apply for an overriding lease? Obviously all the partners could apply together if they have all paid, but what is to stop one of them making a payment and then claiming an overriding lease as sole tenant? There appears to be nothing in the Act to prevent this and it may well be of concern to the landlord who would presumably prefer the overriding lease to be taken in the name of all the partners rather than just one of them.

It may be argued that s. 28(4) requires the tenants to act jointly. It provides that references in the Act to the tenant are references to all the persons who constitute the tenant. However, it takes some effort of construction to apply this definition to s. 17. The argument would be that the s. 17 must be served on a former tenant, i.e., all the persons who constitute the former tenant. In order to demand an overriding lease, payment must be made in accordance with the s. 17 notice. This payment may be made, though, by one of the former tenants and there is nothing in s. 17 or s. 19 to compel a court to hold that such a single person must be held to pay or to claim the overriding lease on behalf of others.

Section 17 provides that a notice may be served on 'a person ("the former tenant")'. There appears to be nothing in the Act to prevent one joint tenant from constituting 'a person' for the purposes of s. 17 and having the right to apply for an overriding lease.

This can be contrasted with the position under the Landlord and Tenant Act 1954 where there are special provisions relating to the renewal of partnership leases where some of the original partner tenants are no longer partners, e.g., they have retired from or left the partnership (see the Landlord and Tenant Act 1954, s. 41). If the partners do not rely on these provisions then all of the original tenants must apply for the new lease (see *Jacobs* v *Chaudhuri* [1968] 2 QB 470). This is the position under s. 19 of the 1995 Act.

A similar situation to that arising under s. 17 arose in respect of statutory protection under the Rent Act 1968 in the case of *Lloyd* v *Sadler* [1978] QB 774. A landlord had let a flat on a protected tenancy to two joint tenants. After one of them had left, never to return, and the term had come to an end the landlord sought possession. The joint tenant who remained claimed that she was protected under the Rent Act. The relevant section of the Act stated that:

> . . . after the termination of a protected tenancy of a dwelling house the person who, immediately before that termination, was the protected tenant of the dwelling house shall, if and so long as he occupies the dwelling house as his residence, be the statutory tenant of it.

The landlord's appeal against the trial judge's refusal of possession was refused and the Court of Appeal held that the ordinary law relating to joint tenancies was not to be applied to the section in its full strictness and that, having regard to the intention of Parliament when the Act was passed, the phrase 'the tenant', where there was a joint tenancy, was to be read as meaning either both the joint tenants or any one or more of them. Interestingly it was said by Megaw LJ that there had never been anything in the Rent Acts expressly dealing with joint tenants or joint tenancies and indeed the relevant provisions in the Rent Act 1977 are identical to those in the 1968 Act. It seems that Parliament has also overlooked joint tenants in s. 17 of the 1995 Act.

So by analogy it appears possible to argue that the phrase 'a person ("the former tenant")' in s. 17 allows one of a number of joint tenants who has paid the sum claimed in the s. 17 notice to claim an overriding lease. Whether Parliament will step in as it did to amend the 1954 Act remains to be seen. In the meantime any attempt by a landlord to restrict a joint tenant's right to apply for an overriding lease will be caught by the anti-avoidance provisions in the 1995 Act.

Lease renewals

Renewal of leases under 1954 Act

Renewals of business leases under part II of the Landlord and Tenant Act 1954 on or after 1 January 1996 will be new tenancies for the purposes of the 1995 Act unless they have been renewed pursuant to a court order which was made before that date (s. 1). A lease which has been entered into pursuant to a pre-Act court order should contain a statement to that effect so that there can be no doubt about its status (see page 6). It would appear that on a subsequent renewal such a lease will become a new tenancy as it will not then be renewed pursuant to a pre-Act court order.

Rent payable under a renewal tenancy

The rent which is payable under a tenancy which has been renewed under part II of the Landlord and Tenant Act 1954 is determined in accordance with s. 34 of that Act. This provides that the rent will be such as may be agreed between the parties, or if they cannot agree, such rent as the court determines is the rent which, having regard to the terms of the tenancy, other than those relating to rent, the holding might reasonably be expected to be let at in the open market by a willing lessor, disregarding the four factors set out in s. 34(1).

The 1995 Act, sch. 1, para. 3, amends s. 34 by inserting a new subsection (4) which provides that the court must, when determining the rent, take into account any effect on rent of the operation of the provisions of the 1995 Act. The effect of this provision is that the court, when setting the new rent, must take into account the effect of the removal of privity of contract and as a result the landlord may be awarded an increase in the rent to compensate for this loss.

Can a renewal lease include conditions governing the landlord's right to give consent to assignments or other new terms?

Under s. 35 of the Landlord and Tenant Act 1954 the terms of the renewal lease (other than the duration and the rent) are to be agreed by the landlord and the tenant, and, in default, will be decided by the court having regard to the terms of the current tenancy and to all the relevant circumstances.

The attitude of the courts is governed by the decision of the House of Lords in *O'May* v *City of London Real Property Co. Ltd* [1983] 2 AC 726. In this case the landlord of a five-year lease of an office on the fifth floor wanted to include in the renewal lease an obligation for the tenant to pay a share of the cost of structural repairs, lift maintenance and repair, and the provision of a sinking fund. This was to be done by way of a variable service charge and would have meant that the lease terms would have to be changed as the original lease included a fixed service charge. It was shown that it was normal at that time to include such service charges in order to provide a 'clear lease' which would be acceptable to institutional buyers.

It was held that the party who is proposing a change to the lease must show that the change is fair and reasonable in all the circumstances. On the facts the landlord had not shown that there should be a departure from the original terms as, first, the variation required the tenant to take on the risk of an unpredictable liability which was disproportionate to its interest and, secondly, the tenant would have no control over the work which it would have to pay for.

The effect of the decision is to protect a tenant from commercial reality.

However, s. 35 of the 1954 Act is amended by sch. 1, para. 4 of this Act. The effect is that the operation of this Act is one of the relevant circumstances in settling the new lease terms. The landlord now has to show that the terms requested have become usual terms as a result of the 1995 Act. It is suggested that as a result a landlord will be able to have included a requirement that the tenant enters into an AGA on assignment.

Rent review

Existing leases

An existing lease, and those which are completed on or after 1 January 1996 but which are not new tenancies, will have continuing tenant liability and this should have the effect of depressing the rent on review. From the point of view of a landlord a lease which is subject to the 1995 Act will be more favourable on rent review than one which is not subject to the Act. A landlord may, therefore, seek the tenant's agreement to amend the rent review clause in an existing lease so that the hypothetical lease becomes a new tenancy under the Act.

Such an amendment should be strongly resisted by a tenant as there is no reason why a tenant would want such a provision in the rent review procedure. However, it may be possible that such an amendment may be agreed to by a prospective assignee but it should be borne in mind that a landlord who withholds consent to assign a lease until such a provision is agreed to will be acting unreasonably. It is also arguable that such a variation is caught by the anti-avoidance provisions in s. 25 as it could be construed as an attempt to 'modify' the application of the Act.

In the remote event that such a variation is agreed to then an assumption will be included in the rent review machinery to the effect that the hypothetical lease will be valued as if it were a new tenancy under s. 1 (see appendix 4).

In any event the hypothetical lease will *prima facie* be valued as a new lease if its *hypothetical* commencement date is after 1995. A tenant may argue, though, that the notorious 'presumption in favour of reality' requires the real old lease to be valued as a hypothetical old lease (see the *Broadgate Square cases* [1995] 1 EG 111).

New leases

There is nothing in general terms about the 1995 Act which is disadvantageous to a tenant and so there is no reason why in a new lease the Act should be disregarded as rent review.

A landlord may wish that no account is taken on a rent review of the tight restrictions on assignment which have been included in the lease, nor of the fact that the tenant is required to enter into an AGA on assigning the lease. This can be done by including assumptions in the rent review machinery that:

(a)   the tenant does not require the landlord's consent to assign, and

(b)   the tenant is not required to enter into an AGA on assigning the lease.

See appendix 4 for examples of such assumptions.

Alternatively, the usual assumption in rent review machinery that the hypothetical lease is on the same terms as the lease except for the amount of the rent could be amended so that in addition to the rent the provisions in the lease dealing with assignment are also excluded. The effect of such a clause will then be that the hypothetical lease will contain no provisions relating to assignment and the tenant will be free to assign it at will without the landlord's consent.

The effect of these assumptions will cause the tenant to suffer on a rent review as they will increase the rent. A tenant's solicitor should consider resisting their inclusion so that the tenant can take the benefit of the restrictions to which the lease is subject. A compromise, if appropriate, where there are tight restrictions on assignment in the lease might be to assume that the hypothetical lease contains a covenant by the tenant not to assign the lease without the consent of the landlord, such consent not to be unreasonably withheld (see appendix 4).

An alternative to these assumptions would be to deal with these matters by way of disregards. In other words, there will on a rent review be disregarded, first, any effect on the rent due to the restrictions on assignment contained in the lease and, secondly, due to the fact that the tenant may be required to enter into an AGA (see appendix 4). Where the previous tenant has entered into an AGA it will affect the rent and the landlord should seek to have this effect disregarded as well.

A tenant may seek to include a provision in the rent review machinery whereby the hypothetical lease is not a new tenancy under s. 1. Such a clause may be caught by the anti-avoidance provisions in s. 25 and, therefore, may be void.

Incorporation of the statutory disregards

Existing leases

Some leases incorporate the disregards contained in the Landlord and Tenant Act 1954, s. 34, rather than expressly setting out the matters which are to be disregarded on a rent review. The usual form of wording used to incorporate these statutory disregards is: 'disregarding the matters contained in the Landlord and Tenant Act 1954, s. 34(1)'. Where this form of wording is used the new subsection (4) which is inserted into s. 34 by the 1995 Act will have no effect. However, in some poorly drafted leases the wording used may just say that the matters which are to be disregarded are those matters contained in s. 34. This would then have the effect of disregarding the matters contained in s. 34(4) on a rent review, i.e., the effect on the rent of the 1995 Act. It is suggested by Murray Ross, *Drafting and Negotiating Commercial Leases*, 4th ed. (London: Butterworths, 1994) at p. 108 that the effect of such wording may in fact be to require the matters contained in s. 34 to be regarded on rent review.

Having said this the question does arise whether the reference to s. 34 is to s. 34 as it was when the lease in question was completed or to the section as amended by the 1995 Act. It may be specifically stated in the rent review provisions that the reference to s. 34 is to the section as subsequently amended. If it does not then the authorities are not clear on the position, see *Euston Centre Properties Ltd* v *H. & J. Wilson Ltd* (1981) 262 EG 1079 and *Brett* v *Brett Essex Golf Club Ltd* [1986] 1 EGLR 154.

New leases

It is not advisable to incorporate s. 34 when drafting rent review provisions and this style of drafting should not be used in connection with new leases. The reasons are discussed by Ross, *Drafting and Negotiating Commercial Leases*, 4th ed., pp 108–9.

Rent deposit bonds

It has become not uncommon for rent deposit bonds to be used to protect a landlord from default by a tenant. A rent deposit bond may guarantee the payment of rent for a certain period. There is a possibility of such bonds being affected by the 1995 Act because s. 24(2) provides that:

> Where—
>
> . . .
>
> (b)   immediately before the release [of a tenant] another person is bound by a covenant of the tenancy imposing any liability or penalty in the event of a failure to comply with that tenant covenant,
>
> then, as from the release of the tenant, that other person is released from the covenant . . . to the same extent.

This means that if the covenant in the rent deposit is a covenant of the tenancy then the covenantor will be released when the tenant is released.

Section 28(1) provides that:

> 'covenant' includes term, condition and obligation, and references to a covenant (or any description of covenant) of a tenancy include a covenant (or a covenant of that description) contained in a collateral agreement.

It seems clear from this that the guarantee contained in a rent deposit bond is released when the tenant is released. Not uncommonly the rent deposit bond may be for a number of years' rent and so, on an earlier release of the tenant, there will be an earlier release of the bond.

The Tyneside Flat Scheme

The Tyneside Flat Scheme is a typical one used to facilitate the conveyancing of pairs of terraced maisonettes, which are known locally as Tyneside flats. Under this scheme the steps are as follows:

(a) One of the flats in the pair is leased to T1 for 999 years at a peppercorn rent. In this lease the freeholder promises that, when granting a lease of the other flat, the freeholder will:

(i) transfer the freehold of that second flat to the tenant of the first flat, and

(ii) transfer the freehold of the first flat to the tenant of the second flat.

(b) When the second flat is sold, a lease is granted by the freeholder containing similar covenants to the first lease and the freeholds are then transferred in accordance with the above.

(c) After both leases are set up, the scheme is then that each tenant will on a sale assign the lease of that flat to the buyer together with the freehold reversion to the other flat in the scheme.

How does the 1995 Act apply to this scheme?

Both leases are granted before 1 January 1996

After transferring the reversions following the sale of the second flat, the freeholder will remain liable on the covenants which run with the reversion (LPA 1925, s. 142).

The first lease is granted before 1 January 1996

If the first lease is granted before 1 January 1996 but the second is granted on or after, the freeholder will be able to apply to be released under s. 6 in relation to liability under the second lease. The freeholder cannot apply in relation to the first lease as this will not be a 'new tenancy'. The tenant of the second lease will be automatically released under s. 5.

The contingent liability of the original tenant of an old tenancy under the tenant covenants will remain unless expressly released.

Both leases are granted on or after 1 January 1996

Each lease will be a 'new tenancy' and so, on the transfer of the reversions, the original freeholder can apply to be released under s. 6 and each tenant will be automatically released on assignment under s. 5.

It would seem a sensible variation of the flat scheme to include a provision in the original lease that when the freehold is assigned the original freeholder will be released by the existing tenant from contingent liability. It appears clear that s. 25(1) of the Act prevents such a provision being included in the original lease. Section 25(1) states that any agreement is void which modifies the operation of the 1995 Act and an agreement binding a tenant to agree to a release must be a forbidden modification of the Act's scheme.

The result of this is that the freeholder's contingent liability to perform the landlord covenants will remain until the end of the lease.

So far as the tenants are concerned the Act will apply in the normal way and each will be released upon assignment. This will be so, of course, only if the lease is a new tenancy within the 1995 Act (i.e., one granted after 1995). In a number of cases this will mean that one tenant is holding under a new tenancy with the benefit of automatic release and one under an old tenancy without his benefit.

Registered Conveyancing New Rules

The Land Registration (No. 3) Rules 1995 (reproduced in appendix 3) prescribe new forms for transfers of registered leasehold land for:

(a)   Transfers of land subject to a rentcharge.

(b)   Transfers of 'old leases' already registered.

(c)   Transfers of 'new leases' already registered.

(d)   Transfers of registered leases where the rent is apportioned or some land exonerated from the rent.

4

Alienation Clauses

At common law a tenant is entitled to assign or underlet the premises in the absence of a covenant in the lease preventing this (*Keeves* v *Dean* [1924] 1 KB 685 at p. 691; *Leith Properties Ltd* v *Byrne* [1983] QB 433). A lease will therefore usually include a covenant against alienation so that the landlord can control the tenant's right to assign or underlet. A usual form for such a covenant is to prevent the tenant from dealing with a part of the premises but to allow an assignment or underletting of the whole of the premises with the landlord's consent, which is not to be unreasonably withheld.

Absolute covenants

An absolute covenant prevents the tenant from dealing with the property in any way, and in the absence of consent by the landlord to carry out a particular transaction an assignment or underletting by the tenant will be in breach of covenant (see page 45).

Qualified covenants

A qualified covenant is one which prevents the tenant from dealing with the property without the landlord's consent. However, it is usual to make the covenant fully qualified by providing that this consent shall not be unreasonably withheld.

There are a number of statutory provisions affecting qualified covenants and these are contained in the LPA 1925, the Landlord and Tenant Act 1927 and the Landlord and Tenant Act 1988.

Landlord's consent not to be unreasonably withheld

Section 19(1)(a) of the Landlord and Tenant Act 1927 provides that, except in the case of building leases and notwithstanding any express provision in the lease to the contrary, a qualified covenant against assigning, underletting, charging or parting with possession of the whole or any part of the property is deemed to be subject to a proviso that consent is not to be unreasonably withheld. The section is set out in full in appendix 2. The effect of s. 19 is to turn a qualified covenant into a fully qualified one. A landlord cannot therefore withhold consent unless there are reasonable grounds for doing so.

A landlord cannot, except as mentioned below, attempt to exclude s. 19(1)(a) by stipulating in the lease the circumstances in which it will be reasonable for the landlord to refuse consent (see *Re Smith's Lease, Smith* v *Richards* [1951] 1 All ER 346). However, the landlord can specify limits on the grounds for refusal, e.g., that consent will not be refused in the case of a respectable or responsible person, which will mean that the landlord cannot refuse consent if the tenant wishes to assign or sublet to a person who fulfils this requirement (*Moat* v *Martin* [1950] 1 KB 175).

A way in which a landlord can seek to avoid the requirements of s. 19(1)(a) is by the use of 'a surrender back' or '*Adler*' clause (*Adler* v *Upper Grosvenor Street Investment Ltd* [1957] 1 WLR 227; approved in *Bocardo SA* v *S and M Hotels Ltd* [1980] 1 WLR 17). The effect of such a clause is to make the operation of the fully qualified covenant subject to the tenant first offering the lease to the landlord by way of a surrender. If the landlord refuses the surrender then the covenant comes into play. The problem with such a clause is that if the lease is subject to part II of the Landlord and Tenant Act 1954 and the landlord accepts the offer of surrender, this agreement will be void under s. 38(1) of the Act (see *Allnatt London Properties Ltd* v *Newton* [1984] 1 All ER 423). However, this problem will not arise if the lease is contracted out of the Act. In its report (Law Com No. 141) the Law Commission recommended the abolition of such clauses in most tenancies.

Two views on the restrictions which can be added to an alienation clause have been put forward by Murray Ross in *Drafting and Negotiating Commercial Leases*, 4th ed. (London: Butterworths, 1994). The first of these is a narrow view in which such restrictions are not subject to the test of reasonableness provided that they are preconditions to the coming into operation of the alienation covenant. The other is a wider view that they are vulnerable only if they expressly purport to specify what will or will not be considered to be reasonable, or when the landlord will or will not be considered to be unreasonably withholding consent.

Section 19 does not apply to leases of agricultural holdings (s. 19(4)).

Reasonableness

The Court of Appeal in the case of *International Drilling Fluids Ltd* v *Louisville Investments (Uxbridge) Ltd* [1986] Ch 513 laid down seven principles gathered from the authorities which are to be used in deciding whether a landlord's refusal is reasonable. The last of these is that, subject to the first six principles, each case is to be considered on its own facts and circumstances. The principles are as follows:

(a) the purpose of a fully qualified covenant is to protect the landlord from having the premises used or occupied in an undesirable way, or by an undesirable tenant or assignee;

(b) a landlord is not entitled to refuse consent on grounds which have nothing to do with the relationship of landlord and tenant in regard to the subject matter of the lease;

(c) it is not necessary for the landlord to prove that the conclusions which led to the refusal of consent were justified, provided that they are conclusions which a reasonable man might have reached in the circumstances;

(d) it may be reasonable to refuse consent on the ground of the proposed use, even if it is not expressly prohibited by the lease;

(e) it may be unreasonable to refuse consent if the refusal will cause harm to the tenant which is disproportionate to the resulting benefit to the landlord;

(f) subject to the above, the reasonableness of a refusal is a question of fact to be decided in the light of all the circumstances.

These principles have subsequently been applied in *Tollbench Ltd* v *Plymouth City Council* (1988) 56 P & CR 194 and *Orlando Investments Ltd* v *Grosvenor Estate Belgravia* (1989) 59 P & CR 21. In the first of these cases it was decided that a landlord can only rely on reasons which actually influenced him at the time that he withheld his consent.

Examples of reasonable refusal

The following have been held to be reasonable grounds for refusing consent:

(a)   Unsatisfactory references have been provided in respect of the proposed assignee (*Shanly* v *Ward* (1913) 29 TLR 714; *Rossi* v *Hestdrive Ltd* [1985] 1 EGLR 50).

(b)   The landlord has serious doubts about the proposed assignee's ability to pay the rent or to comply with the repairing covenant in the lease (see *Ponderosa International Development Inc.* v *Pengap Securities (Bristol) Ltd* [1986] 1 EGLR 66; *British Bakeries (Midlands) Ltd* v *Michael Testler and Co. Ltd* [1986] 1 EGLR 64).

(c)   The landlord considers that other property which he owns will be affected by the assignee's proposed use of the premises (*Governors of Bridewell Hospital* v *Fawkner and Rogers* (1892) 8 TLR 637).

(d)   There are breaches of the repair covenant and the landlord is not satisfied that the assignee will remedy them (*Orlando Investments Ltd* v *Grosvenor Estate Belgravia* (1989) 59 P & CR 21).

(e)   The assignment will reduce the rent by half (*Olympia and York Canary Wharf Ltd* v *Oil Property Investment Ltd* (1994) 69 P & Cr 43).

(f)   The assignee's proposed use of the premises will be in breach of a covenant in the lease (*F.W. Woolworth plc* v *Charlwood Alliance Properties Ltd* [1987] 1 EGLR 53).

(g)   The value of the property will be reduced (*Re Town Investments Ltd's Underlease* [1954] Ch 301).

(h)   The assignee will have the right to enfranchise under statute (*Norfolk Capital Group Ltd* v *Kitway Ltd* [1977] QB 506; *Bickel* v *Duke of Westminster* [1977] QB 517), which would clearly apply to a right under the Leasehold Reform Housing and Urban Development Act 1993.

(i)   The proposed transaction will alter the nature of the tenancy from a business tenancy to a mixed business and residential use (*West Layton Ltd* v *Ford* [1979] QB 593).

Examples of unreasonable refusal

The following are examples of circumstances in which a landlord's refusal of consent was not upheld:

(a)   Where the landlord has ignored the financial standing of a proposed guarantor (*Venetian Glass Gallery Ltd* v *Next Properties Ltd* [1989] 2 EGLR 42).

(b)   Where the landlord's sole reason for refusing consent was to obtain possession of the premises (*Bates* v *Donaldson* [1986] 2 QB 241).

(c)   Where a superior landlord might unreasonably withhold consent (*Vienit Ltd* v *W. Williams and Son (Bread Street) Ltd* [1958] 1 WLR 1267).

(d)   Where an undertenant was required to covenant directly with the landlord for the payment of the rent reserved in the lease (*Balfour* v *Kensington Gardens Mansions Ltd* (1932) 49 TLR 29).

(e)   Where the landlord objected to an assignment because future subtenancies might give rise to management problems (*Rayburn* v *Wolf* (1985) 50 P & CR 463).

(f)   Where there was a minor breach of the repairing covenant and the assignee intended to spend a large amount of money on repairs (*Farr* v *Ginnings* (1928) 44 TLR 249).

Consent cannot be withheld on the grounds of race or sex. Section 24 of the Race Relations Act 1976 provides that it is unlawful to discriminate on the grounds of race by withholding consent. However, this does not apply if the person withholding consent, or a near relative, resides and intends to continue to reside on the premises, there is shared accommodation and the premises are 'small premises' (defined in s. 22(2)). It is also unlawful to discriminate on the grounds of sex by withholding consent (Sex Discrimination Act 1975, s. 31).

A recent example of an unreasonable refusal by a landlord is *Kened Ltd* v *Connie Investments Ltd* (1995) 70 P & CR 370. In this case the landlord refused to consent to the assignment of a lease of a hotel on the grounds, first, that the proposed assignee's covenant was of little or no value and, secondly, that the proposed assignee's surety did not have adequate assets in England for it to comply with the assignee's covenant in the lease. The proposed assignee was a company which had been formed specifically for purchasing hotels. Its surety was its parent company which had substantial assets but was registered abroad where it carried on its business. At first instance it was held that the landlord had unreasonably withheld its consent.

This decision was upheld by the Court of Appeal which said that the trial judge had applied the correct test which was that it had to be shown that no reasonable landlord would have withheld consent. This was an objective test and on the facts before him the judge reached a decision he was entitled to reach. The landlord was not entitled to particulars of the assignment and of any premium or reverse premium which was to be paid. All that he was concerned with is the identity and character of the proposed assignee.

Payment for consent

A landlord may not require the payment of a fine for giving consent unless there is express provision in the lease (LPA 1925, s. 144). However, there is nothing to prevent a landlord from requiring payment of a reasonable amount in respect of legal or other expenses in relation to giving the consent.

Leases do exist where s. 144 has been excluded. This amounts to a trap for the tenant as this exclusion can easily be overlooked. The effect of such a term can be catastrophic for the tenant who may be required to pay a sum of money for assigning the lease which could amount to a 'ransom'.

Statutory duties imposed on the landlord

The Landlord and Tenant Act 1988 imposes statutory duties on a landlord who receives an application for consent to assign, underlet, charge or part with possession of the premises. Its purpose is to prevent undue delay on the part of a landlord. A breach of any of the statutory duties in the Act gives rise to an action for the tort of breach of statutory duty, the remedy for which will be damages.

Section 1(3) of the 1988 Act provides that where a tenant serves a written application for consent on the landlord, the landlord owes a duty to the tenant, within a reasonable time:

    (a) to give consent, except in a case where it is reasonable not to give consent,

    (b) to serve on the tenant written notice of his decision whether or not to give consent specifying in addition—

        (i) if the consent is given subject to conditions, the conditions,

(ii)   if the consent is withheld, the reasons for withholding it.

A landlord is also under a duty to pass the application on to any other person whose consent is required, e.g., a superior landlord (s. 2) who will then owe a similar duty (s. 3).

There is no definition in the 1988 Act of what will be a reasonable time for responding to the tenant's request. The Law Commission in 1985 suggested a 28-day period (*Covenants Restricting Dispositions, Alterations and Change of User* (Law Com No. 141)). In *Midland Bank plc* v *Chart Enterprises Inc.* [1990] 2 EGLR 59 a period of 10 weeks between the tenant applying for consent and the landlord giving notice of its decision was held to be unreasonable. Recently in *Dong Bang Minerva (UK) Ltd* v *Davina Ltd* [1995] 1 EGLR 41 it was suggested that 28 days would be a reasonable time for a landlord to reply to a tenant's request for consent. This case involved consent to a proposed underlease and it was said that a landlord might reasonably delay giving consent until sufficient particulars of the proposed underlease had been received for a decision to be made on its merits. This can be contrasted with *Kened Ltd* v *Connie Investments Ltd* (1995) 70 P & CR 370 where the landlord was not entitled to particulars of the proposed assignment. The court in *Dong Bang Minerva (UK) Ltd* v *Davina Ltd* did not rule on whether it would be reasonable for the landlord to delay until receiving an undertaking to pay reasonable costs.

The application of the Landlord and Tenant Act 1988 was also considered in *Olympia and York Canary Wharf Ltd* v *Oil Property Investment Ltd* (1994) 69 P & CR 43. In this case the current tenants were seeking consent to assign the lease back to the original tenant so that the latter could exercise a personal right in the lease to bring it to an end at the end of the tenth year of the term. The landlord had refused consent as it did not want this right to be exercised. The current tenants were in administration and the original tenant had been paying the rent, which was double the current market rent, for some time. The current tenants argued that by refusing consent the landlord was stopping the operation of a benefit in the lease and that the refusal was unreasonable. The Court of Appeal rejected this argument on the basis that the benefit had been conferred on the original tenant personally and that it had been lost when the lease had been assigned, though it could come back into existence should the lease be assigned back to the original tenant. There was no such right between the landlord and the current tenants and it was clear that the only reason for the proposed assignment was so that the lease could be brought to an end. The landlord was therefore reasonable in refusing its consent.

The onus is on the landlord to prove that any condition imposed is reasonable and that if consent is refused it was reasonable to do so (Landlord and Tenant Act 1988, ss. 1(6) and 3(5)). In *Air India* v *Balabel* [1993] 2 EGLR 66 the Court of Appeal confirmed that the Landlord and Tenant Act 1988 had not altered the law as stated by Balcombe LJ in *International Drilling Fluids Ltd* v *Louisville Investments (Uxbridge) Ltd* [1986] Ch 513 that it is not necessary for the landlord to prove that the conclusions which led him to refuse consent were justified, provided that they are conclusions which a reasonable man might have reached in the circumstances.

A landlord cannot prove that a refusal of consent was reasonable by relying on matters which did not influence him at the time of refusal (see *CIN Properties Ltd* v *Gill* [1993] 2 EGLR 97 where the landlord could not rely on events which had taken place after it had refused consent in order to prove that it had reasonably refused consent).

Building leases

Before 1 January 1996

A building lease is a lease which is made in consideration, either wholly or partially, of the erection or substantial improvement, alteration or addition of buildings.

Alienation clauses in building leases are dealt with by the Landlord and Tenant Act 1927, s. 19(1)(b). This provides that, in the case of a building lease which has been granted for more than 40 years, a tenant may, notwithstanding a covenant preventing assignment without the landlord's consent, assign the lease without the landlord's consent provided that the assignment is made more than seven years before the end of the term, and that, within six months of completion of the assignment, notice is given to the landlord.

Section 19(1)(b) does not apply where the landlord is a government department, a local or public authority, or a statutory or public utility company.

A building lease may include a covenant which provides that the landlord is entitled to require the assignee to provide an acceptable guarantor and to enter into a covenant to observe the covenants in the lease for the remainder of the term. Such provisions may be enforced by the landlord (see *Vaux Group plc* v *Lilley* [1991] 1 EGLR 60).

On or after 1 January 1996

Section 22 of the 1995 Act amends the Landlord and Tenant Act 1927, s. 19, by providing that in relation to a qualifying lease s. 19(1)(b) will not apply. This means that a building lease which is a new tenancy and which is not a residential lease will now be subject to the new law and so the landlord's consent will be needed throughout the whole of the term of the lease where there is a qualified covenant against assignment.

A building lease which is of residential property is not caught by this amendment and so will still be subject to the pre-Act law.

Appendix 1

Text of the Landlord and Tenant (Covenants) Act 1995

1995   CHAPTER 30

ARRANGEMENTS OF SECTIONS

Preliminary

An Act to make provision for persons bound by covenants of a tenancy to be released from such covenants on the assignment of the tenancy, and to make other provision with respect to rights and liabilities arising under such covenants; to restrict in certain circumstances the operation of rights of re-entry, forfeiture and disclaimer; and for connected purposes.

[19th July 1995]

Preliminary

1. Tenancies to which the Act applies

(1)   Sections 3 to 16 and 21 apply only to new tenancies.

(2)   Sections 17 to 20 apply to both new and other tenancies.

(3)   For the purposes of this section a tenancy is a new tenancy if it is granted on or after the date on which this Act comes into force otherwise than in pursuance of—

(a)   an agreement entered into before that date, or

(b)   an order of a court made before that date.

(4)   Subsection (3) has effect subject to section 20(1) in the case of overriding leases granted under section 19.

(5)   Without prejudice to the generality of subsection (3), that subsection applies to the grant of a tenancy where by virtue of any variation of a tenancy there is a deemed surrender and regrant as it applies to any other grant of a tenancy.

(6)   Where a tenancy granted on or after the date on which this Act comes into force is so granted in pursuance of an option granted before that date, the tenancy shall be regarded for the purposes of subsection (3) as granted in pursuance of an agreement entered into before that date (and accordingly is not a new tenancy), whether or not the option was exercised before that date.

(7)   In subsection (6) 'option' includes the right of first refusal.

2. Covenants to which the Act applies

(1)   This Act applies to a landlord covenant or a tenant covenant of a tenancy—

(a)   whether or not the covenant has reference to the subject matter of the tenancy, and

(b)   whether the covenant is express, implied or imposed by law, but does not apply to a covenant falling within subsection (2).

(2)   Nothing in this Act affects any covenant imposed in pursuance of—

(a)   section 35 or 155 of the Housing Act 1985 (covenants for repayment of discount on early disposals);

(b)   paragraph 1 of Schedule 6A to that Act (covenants requiring redemption of landlord's share); or

(c)   paragraph 1 or 3 of Schedule 2 to the Housing Associations Act 1985 (covenants for repaying of discount on early disposals or for restricting disposals).

Transmission of covenants

3.   Transmission of benefit and burden of covenants

(1)   The benefit and burden of all landlord and tenant covenants of a tenancy—

(a)   shall be annexed and incident to the whole, and to each and every part, of the premises demised by the tenancy and of the reversion in them, and

(b)   shall in accordance with this section pass on an assignment of the whole or any part of those premises or of the reversion in them.

(2)   Where the assignment is by the tenant under the tenancy, then as from the assignment the assignee—

(a)   becomes bound by the tenant covenants of the tenancy except to the extent that—

(i)   immediately before the assignment they did not bind the assignor, or

(ii)   they fall to be complied with in relation to any demised premises not comprised in the assignment; and

(b)   becomes entitled to the benefit of the landlord covenants of the tenancy except to the extent that they fall to be complied with in relation to any such premises.

(3)   Where the assignment is by the landlord under the tenancy, then as from the assignment the assignee—

(a)   becomes bound by the landlord covenants of the tenancy except to the extent that—

(i)   immediately before the assignment they did not bind the assignor, or

(ii)   they fall to be complied with in relation to any demised premises not comprised in the assignment; and

(b)   becomes entitled to the benefit of the tenant covenants of the tenancy except to the extent that they fall to be complied with in relation to any such premises.

(4)   In determining for the purposes of subsection (2) or (3) whether any covenant bound the assignor immediately before the assignment, any waiver or release of the covenant which (in whatever terms) is expressed to be personal to the assignor shall be disregarded.

(5)   Any landlord or tenant covenant of a tenancy which is restrictive of the user of land shall, as well as being capable of enforcement against an

assignee, be capable of being enforced against any other person who is the owner or occupier of any demised premises to which the covenant relates, even though there is no express provision in the tenancy to that effect.

(6)   Nothing in this section shall operate—

(a)   in the case of a covenant which (in whatever terms) is expressed to be personal to any person, to make the covenant enforceable by or (as the case may be) against any other person; or

(b)   to make a covenant enforceable against any person if, apart from this section, it would not be enforceable against him by reason of its not having been registered under the Land Registration Act 1925 or the Land Charges Act 1972.

(7)   To the extent that there remains in force any rule of law by virtue of which the burden of a covenant whose subject matter is not in existence at the time when it is made does not run with the land affected unless the covenantor covenants on behalf of himself and his assigns, that rule of law is hereby abolished in relation to tenancies.

4.   Transmission of rights of re-entry

The benefit of a landlord's right of re-enry under a tenancy—

(a)   shall be annexed and incident to the whole, and to each and every part, of the reversion in the premises demised by the tenancy, and

(b)   shall pass on an assignment of the whole or any part of the reversion in those premises.

Release of covenants on assignment

5.   Tenant released from covenants on assignment of tenancy

(1)   This section applies where a tenant assigns premises demised to him under a tenancy.

(2)   If the tenant assigns the whole of the premises demised to him, he—

(a)   is released from the tenant covenants of the tenancy, and

(b)   ceases to be entitled to the benefit of the landlord covenants of the tenancy,

as from the assignment.

(3)   If the tenant assigns part only of the premises demised to him, then as from the assignment he—

(a)   is released from the tenant covenants of the tenancy, and

(b)   ceases to be entitled to the benefit of the landlord covenants of the tenancy,

only to the extent that those covenants fall to be complied with in relation to that part of the demised premises.

(4)   This section applies as mentioned in subsection (1) whether or not the tenant is tenant of the whole of the premises comprised in the tenancy.

6. Landlord may be released from covenants on assignment of reversion

(1) This section applies where a landlord assigns the reversion in premises of which he is the landlord under a tenancy.

(2) If the landlord assigns the reversion in the whole of the premises of which he is the landlord—

(a) he may apply to be released from the landlord covenants of the tenancy in accordance with section 8; and

(b) if he is so released from all of those covenants, he ceases to be entitled to the benefit of the tenant covenants of the tenancy as from the assignment.

(3) If the landlord assigns the reversion in part only of the premises of which he is landlord—

(a) he may apply to be so released from the landlord covenants of the tenancy to the extent that they fall to be complied with in relation to that part of those premises; and

(b) if he is, to that extent, so released from all of those covenants, then as from the assignment he ceases to be entitled to the benefit of the tenant covenants only to the extent that they fall to be complied with in relation to that part of those premises.

(4) This section applies as mentioned in subsection (1) whether or not the landlord is landlord of the whole of the premises comprised in the tenancy.

7. Former landlord may be released from covenants on assignment of reversion

(1) This section applies where—

(a) a landlord assigns the reversion in premises of which he is the landlord under a tenancy, and

(b) immediately before the assignment a former landlord of the premises remains bound by a landlord covenant of the tenancy ('the relevant covenant').

(2) If immediately before the assignment the former landlord does not remain the landlord of any other premises demised by the tenancy, he may apply to be released from the relevant covenant in accordance with section 8.

(3) In any other case the former landlord may apply to be so released from the relevant covenant to the extent that it falls to be complied with in relation to any premises comprised in the assignment.

(4) If the former landlord is so released from every landlord covenant by which he remained bound immediately before the assignment, he ceases to be entitled to the benefit of the tenant covenants of the tenancy.

(5) If the former landlord is so released from every such landlord covenant to the extent that it falls to be complied with in relation to any premises comprised in the assignment, he ceases to be entitled to the benefit of the tenant covenants of the tenancy to the extent that they fall to be so complied with.

(6) This section applies as mentioned in subsection (1)—

(a) whether or not the landlord making the assignment is landlord of the whole of the premises comprised in the tenancy; and

(b) whether or not the former landlord has previously applied (whether under section 6 or this section) to be released from the relevant covenant.

8. Procedure for seeking release from a covenant under section 6 or 7

(1) For the purposes of section 6 or 7 an application for the release of a covenant to any extent is made by serving on the tenant, either before or within the period of four weeks beginning with the date of the assignment in question, a notice informing him of—

(a) the proposed assignment or (as the case may be) the fact that the assignment has taken place, and

(b) the request for the covenant to be released to that extent.

(2) Where an application for the release of a covenant is made in accordance with subsection (1), the covenant is released to the extent mentioned in the notice if—

(a) the tenant does not, within the period of four weeks beginning with the day on which the notice is served, serve on the landlord or former landlord a notice in writing objecting to the release, or

(b) the tenant does so serve such a notice but the court, on the application of the landlord or former landlord, makes a declaration that it is reasonable for the covenant to be so released, or

(c) the tenant serves on the landlord or former landlord a notice in writing consenting to the release and, if he has previously served a notice objecting to it, stating that that notice is withdrawn.

(3) Any release from a covenant in accordance with this section shall be regarded as occurring at the time when the assignment in question takes place.

(4) In this section—

(a) 'the tenant' means the tenant of the premises comprised in the assignment in question (or, if different parts of those premises are held under the tenancy by different tenants, each of those tenants);

(b) any reference to the landlord or the former landlord is a reference to the landlord referred to in section 6 or the former landlord referred to in section 7, as the case may be; and

(c) 'the court' means a county court.

Apportionment of liability between assignor and assignee

9. Apportionment of liability under covenants binding both assignor and assignee of tenancy or reversion

(1) This section applies where—

(a) a tenant assigns part only of the premises demised to him by a tenancy;

(b) after the assignment both the tenant and his assignee are to be bound by a non-attributable tenant covenant of the tenancy; and

(c) the tenant and his assignee agree that as from the assignment liability under the covenant is to be apportioned between them in such manner as is specified in the agreement.

(2) This section also applies where—

(a) a landlord assigns the reversion in part only of the premises of which he is the landlord under a tenancy;

(b) after the assignment both the landlord and his assignee are to be bound by a non-attributable landlord covenant of the tenancy; and

(c) the landlord and his assignee agree that as from the assignment liability under the covenant is to be apportioned between them in such manner as is specified in the agreement.

(3) Any such agreement as is mentioned in subsection (1) or (2) may apportion liability in such a way that a party to the agreement is exonerated from all liability under a covenant.

(4) In any case falling within subsection (1) or (2) the parties to the agreement may apply for the apportionment to become binding on the appropriate person in accordance with section 10.

(5) In any such case the parties to the agreement may also apply for the apportionment to become binding on any person (other than the appropriate person) who is for the time being entitled to enforce the covenant in question; and section 10 shall apply in relation to such an application as it applies in relation to an application made with respect to the appropriate person.

(6) For the purposes of this section a covenant is, in relation to an assignment, a 'non-attributable' covenant if it does not fall to be complied with in relation to any premises comprised in the assignment.

(7) In this section 'the appropriate person' means either—

(a) the landlord of the entire premises referred to in subsection (1)(a) (or, if different parts of those premises are held under the tenancy by different landlords, each of those landlords), or

(b) the tenant of the entire premises referred to in subsection (2)(a) (or, if different parts of those premises are held under the tenancy by different tenants, each of those tenants), depending on whether the agreement in question falls within subsection (1) or subsection (2).

10. Procedure for making apportionment bind other party to lease

(1) For the purposes of section 9 the parties to an agreement falling within subsection (1) or (2) of that section apply for an apportionment to become binding on the appropriate person if, either before or within the period of four weeks beginning with the date of the assignment in question, they serve on that person a notice informing him of—

(a) the proposed assignment or (as the case may be) the fact that the assignment has taken place;

(b) the prescribed particulars of the agreement; and

(c) their request that the apportionment should become binding on him.

(2) Where an application for an apportionment to become binding has been made in accordance with subsection (1), the apportionment becomes binding on the appropriate person if—

(a) he does not, within the period of four weeks beginnning with the day on which the notice is served under subsection (1), serve on the parties to the agreement a notice in writing objecting to the apportionment becoming binding on him, or

(b) he does so serve such a notice but the court, on the application of the parties to the agreement, makes a declaration that it is reasonable for the apportionment to become binding on him, or

(c) he serves on the parties to the agreement a notice in writing consenting to the apportionment becoming binding on him and, if he has previously served a notice objecting thereto, stating that the notice is withdrawn.

(3) Where any apportionment becomes binding in accordance with this section, this shall be regarded as occurring at the time when the assignment in question takes place.

(4) In this section—

'the appropriate persons' has the same meaning as in section 9;

'the court' means a county court;

'prescribed' means prescribed by virtue of section 27.

Excluded assignments

11. Assignments in breach of covenant or by operation of law

(1) This section provides for the operation of sections 5 to 10 in relation to assignments in breach of a covenant of a tenancy or assignments by operation of law ('excluded assignments').

(2) In the case of an excluded assignment subsection (2) or (3) of section 5—

(a)   shall not have the effect mentioned in that subsection in relation to the tenant as from that assignment, but

(b)   shall have that effect as from the next assignment (if any) of the premises assigned by him which is not an excluded assignment.

(3)   In the case of an excluded assignment subsection (2) or (3) of section 6 or 7—

(a)   shall not enable the landlord or former landlord to apply for such a release as is mentioned in that subsection as from that assignment, but

(b)   shall apply on the next assignment (if any) of the reversion assigned by the landlord which is not an excluded assignment so as to enable the landlord or former landlord to apply for any such release as from that subsequent assignment.

(4)   Where subsection (2) or (3) of section 6 or 7 does so apply—

(a)   any reference in that section to the assignment (except where it relates to the time as from which the release takes effect) is a reference to the excluded assignment; but

(b)   in that excepted case and in section 8 as it applies in relation to any application under that section made by virtue of subsection (3) above, any reference to the assignment or proposed assignment is a reference to any such subsequent assignment as is mentioned in that subsection.

(5)   In the case of an excluded assignment section 9—

(a)   shall not enable the tenant or landlord and his assignee to apply for an agreed apportionment to become binding in accordance with section 10 as from that assignment, but

(b)   shall apply on the next assignment (if any) of the premises or reversion assigned by the tenant or landlord which is not an excluded assignment so as to enable him and his assignee to apply for such an apportionment to become binding in accordance with section 10 as from that subsequent assignment.

(6)   Where section 9 does so apply—

(a)   any reference in that section to the assignment or the assignee under it is a reference to the excluded assignment and the assignee under that assignment; but

(b)   in section 10 as it applies in relation to any application under section 9 made by virtue of subsection (5) above, any reference to the assignment or proposed assignment is a reference to any such subsequent assignment as is mentioned in that subsection.

(7)   If any such subsequent assignment as is mentioned in subsection (2), (3) or (5) above comprises only part of the premises assigned by the tenant or (as the case may be) only part of the premises the reversion in which was assigned by the landlord on the excluded assignment—

(a)   the relevant provision or provisions of section 5, 6, 7 or 9 shall only have the effect mentioned in that subsection to the extent that the covenants or covenant in question fall or falls to be complied with in relation to that part of those premises; and

(b)   that subsection may accordingly apply on different occasions in relation to different parts of those premises.

Third party covenants

12.   Covenants with management companies etc.

(1)   This section applies where—

(a)   a person other than the landlord or tenant ('the third party') is under a covenant of a tenancy liable (as principal) to discharge any function with respect to all or any of the demised premises ('the relevant function'); and

(b)   that liability is not the liability of a guarantor or any other financial liability referable to the performance or otherwise of a covenant of the tenancy by another party to it.

(2)   To the extent that any covenant of the tenancy confers any rights against the third party with respect to the relevant function, then for the purposes of the transmission of the benefit of the covenant in accordance with this Act it shall be treated as if it were—

(a)   a tenant covenant of the tenancy to the extent that those rights are exercisable by the landlord; and

(b)   a landlord covenant of the tenancy to the extent that those rights are exercisable by the tenant.

(3)   To the extent that any covenant of the tenancy confers any rights exercisable by the third party with respect to the relevant functions, then for the purposes mentioned in subsection (4), it shall be treated as if it were—

(a)   a tenant covenant of the tenancy to the extent that those rights are exercisable against the tenant; and

(b)   a landlord covenant of the tenancy to the extent that those rights are exercisable against the landlord.

(4)   The purposes mentioned in subsection (3) are—

(a)   the transmission of the burden of the covenant in accordance with this Act; and

(b)   any release from, or apportionment of liability in respect of, the covenant in accordance with this Act.

(5)   In relation to the release of the landlord from any covenant which is to be treated as a landlord covenant by virtue of subsection (3), section 8 shall apply as if any reference to the tenant were a reference to the third party.

Joint liability under covenants

13. Covenants binding two or more persons

(1) Where in consequence of this Act two or more persons are bound by the same covenant, they are so bound both jointly and severally.

(2) Subject to section 24(2), where by virtue of this Act—

(a) two or more persons are bound jointly and severally by the same covenant, and

(b) any of the persons so bound is released from the covenant,

the release does not extend to any other of those persons.

(3) For the purpose of providing for contribution between persons who, by virtue of this Act, are bound jointly and severally by a covenant, the Civil Liability (Contribution) Act 1978 shall have effect as if—

(a) liability to a person under a covenant were liability in respect of damage suffered by that person;

(b) references to damage accordingly included a breach of a covenant of a tenancy; and

(c) section 7(2) of that Act were omitted.

14. Abolition of indemnity covenants implied by statute

The following provisions (by virtue of which indemnity covenants are implied on the assignment of a tenancy) shall cease to have effect—

(a) subsections (1)(C) and (D) of section 77 of the Law of Property Act 1925; and

(b) subsections (1)(b) and (2) of section 24 of the Land Registration Act 1925.

Enforcement of covenants

15. Enforcement of covenants

(1) Where any tenant covenant of a tenancy, or any right of re-entry contained in a tenancy, is enforceable by the reversioner in respect of any premises demised by the tenancy, it shall also be so enforceable by—

(a) any person (other than the reversioner) who, as the holder of the immediate reversion in those premises, is for the time being entitled to the rents and profits under the tenancy in respect of those premises, or

(b) any mortgagee in possession of the reversion in those premises who is so entitled.

(2) Where any landlord covenant of a tenancy is enforceable against the reversioner in respect of any premises demised by the tenancy, it shall also be enforceable against any person falling within subsection (1)(a) or (b).

(3) Where any landlord covenant of a tenancy is enforceable by the tenant in respect of any premises demised by the tenancy, it shall also be so

enforceable by any mortgagee in possession of those premises under a mortgage granted by the tenant.

(4)   Where any tenant covenant of a tenancy, or any right of re-entry contained in a tenancy, is enforceable against the tenant in respect of any premises demised by the tenancy, it shall also be so enforceable against any such mortgagee.

(5)   Nothing in this section shall operate—

(a)   in the case of a covenant which (in whatever terms) is expressed to be personal to any person to make the covenant enforceable by or (as the case may be) against any other person; or

(b)   to make a covenant enforceable against any person if, apart from this section, it would not be enforceable against him by reason of its not having been registered under the Land Registration Act 1925 or the Land Charges Act 1972.

(6)   In this section—

'mortgagee' and 'mortgage' include 'chargee' and 'charge' respectively; 'the reversioner', in relation to a tenancy, means the holder for the time being of the interest of the landlord under the tenancy.

Liability of former tenant etc. in respect of covenants

16.   Tenant guaranteeing performance of covenant by assignee

(1)   Where on an assignment a tenant is to any extent released from a tenant covenant of a tenancy by virtue of this Act ('the relevant covenant'), nothing in this Act (and in particular section 25) shall preclude him from entering into an authorised guarantee agreement with respect to the performance of that covenant by the assignee.

(2)   For the purposes of this section an agreement is an authorised guarantee agreement if—

(a)   under it the tenant guarantees the performance of the relevant covenant to any extent by the assignee; and

(b)   it is entered into in the circumstances set out in subsection (3); and

(c)   its provisions conform with subsections (4) and (5).

(3)   Those circumstances are as follows—

(a)   by virtue of a covenant against assignment (whether absolute or qualified) the assignment cannot be effected without the consent of the landlord under the tenancy or some other person;

(b)   any such consent is given subject to a condition (lawfully imposed) that the tenant is to enter into an agreement guaranteeing the performance of the covenant by the assignee; and

(c)   the agreement is entered into by the tenant in pursuance of that condition.

(4)   An agreement is not an authorised guarantee agreement to the extent that it purports—

(a) to impose on the tenant any requirement to guarantee in any way the performance of the relevant covenant by any person other than the assignee; or

(b) to impose on the tenant any liability, restriction or other requirement (of whatever nature) in relation to any time after the assignee is released from that covenant by virtue of this Act.

(5)   Subject to subsection (4), an authorised guarantee agreement may—

(a) impose on the tenant any liability as sole or principal debtor in respect of any obligation owed by the assignee under the relevant covenant;

(b) impose on the tenant liabilities as guarantor in respect of the assignee's performance of that covenant which are no more onerous than those to which he would be subject in the event of his being liable as sole or principal debtor in respect of any obligation owed by the assignee under that covenant;

(c) require the tenant, in the event of the tenancy assigned by him being disclaimed, to enter into a new tenancy of the premises comprised in the assignment—

(i)   whose term expires not later than the term of the tenancy assigned by the tenant, and

(ii)   whose tenant covenants are no more onerous than those of that tenancy;

(d) make provision incidental or supplementary to any provision made by virtue of any of paragraphs (a) to (c).

(6)   Where a person ('the former tenant') is to any extent released from a covenant of a tenancy by virtue of section 11(2) as from an assignment and the assignor under the assignment enters into an authorised guarantee agreement with the landlord with respect to the performance of that covenant by the assignee under the assignment—

(a) the landlord may require the former tenant to enter into an agreement under which he guarantees, on terms corresponding to those of that authorised guarantee agreement, the performance of that covenant by the assignee under the assignment; and

(b) if its provisions conform with subsections (4) and (5), any such agreement shall be an authorised guarantee agreement for the purposes of this section; and

(c) in the application of this section in relation to any such agreement—

(i)   subsections (2)(b) and (c) and (3) shall be omitted, and

(ii)   any reference to the tenant or to the assignee shall be read as a reference to the former tenant or to the assignee under the assignment.

(7)   For the purposes of subsection (1) it is immaterial that—

(a)   the tenant has already made an authorised guarantee agreement in respect of a previous assignment by him of the tenancy referred to in that subsection, it having been subsequently revested in him following a disclaimer on behalf of the previous assignee, or

(b)   the tenancy referred to in that subsection is a new tenancy entered into by the tenant in pursuance of an authorised guarantee agreement;
and in any such case subsections (2) to (5) shall apply accordingly.

(8)   It is hereby declared that the rules of law relating to guarantees (and in particular those relating to the release of sureties) are, subject to its terms, applicable in relation to any authorised guarantee agreement as in relation to any other guarantee agreement.

17.   Restriction on liability of former tenant or his guarantor for rent or service charge etc.

(1)   This section applies where a person ('the former tenant') is as a result of an assignment no longer a tenant under a tenancy but—

(a)   (in the case of a tenancy which is a new tenancy) he has under an authorised guarantee agreement guaranteed the performance by his assignee of a tenant covenant of the tenancy under which any fixed charge is payable; or

(b)   (in the case of any tenancy) he remains bound by such a covenant.

(2)   The former tenant shall not be liable under that agreement or (as the case may be) the covenant to pay any amount in respect of any fixed charge payable under the covenant unless, within the period of six months beginning with the date when the charge becomes due, the landlord serves on the former tenant a notice informing him—

(a)   that the charge is now due; and

(b)   that in respect of the charge the landlord intends to recover from the former tenant such amount as is specified in the notice and (where payable) interest calculated on such basis as is so specified.

(3)   Where a person ('the guarantor') has agreed to guarantee the performance by the former tenant of such a covenant as is mentioned in subsection (1), the guarantor shall not be liable under the agreement to pay any amount in respect of any fixed charge payable under the covenant unless, within the period of six months beginning with the date when the charge becomes due, the landlord serves on the guarantor a notice informing him—

(a)   that the charge is now due; and

(b)   that in respect of the charge the landlord intends to recover from the guarantor such amount as is specified in the notice and (where payable) interest calculated on such basis as is so specified.

(4)   Where the landlord has duly served a notice under subsection (2) or (3), the amount (exclusive of interest) which the former tenant or (as the case may be) the guarantor is liable to pay in respect of the fixed charge in question shall not exceed the amount specified in the notice unless—

(a)   his liability in respect of the charge is subsequently determined to be for a greater amount,

(b)   the notice informed him of the possibility that that liability would be so determined, and

(c)   within the period of three months beginning with the date of the determination, the landlord serves on him a further notice informing him that the landlord intends to recover that greater amount from him (plus interest, where payable).

(5)   For the purposes of subsection (2) or (3) any fixed charge which has become due before the date on which this Act comes into force shall be treated as becoming due on that date; but neither of those subsections applies to any such charge if before that date proceedings have been instituted by the landlord for the recovery from the former tenant of any amount in respect of it.

(6)   In this section—

'fixed charge', in relation to a tenancy, means—

(a)   rent,

(b)   any service charge as defined by section 18 of the Landlord and Tenant Act 1985 (the words 'of a dwelling' being disregarded for this purpose), and

(c)   any amount payable under a tenant covenant of the tenancy providing for the payment of a liquidated sum in the event of a failure to comply with any such covenant;

'landlord', in relation to a fixed charge, includes any person who has a right to enforce payment of the charge.

18.   Restriction of liability of former tenant or his guarantor where tenancy subsequently varied

(1)   This section applies where a person ('the former tenant') is as a result of an assignment no longer a tenant under a tenancy but—

(a)   (in the case of a new tenancy) he has under an authorised guarantee agreement guaranteed the performance by his assignee of any tenant covenant of the tenancy; or

(b)   (in the case of any tenancy) he remains bound by such a covenant.

(2)   The former tenant shall not be liable under the agreement or (as the case may be) the covenant to pay any amount in respect of the covenant to the extent that the amount is referable to any relevant variation of the tenant covenants of the tenancy effected after the assignment.

(3) Where a person ('the guarantor') has agreed to guarantee the performance by the former tenant of a tenant covenant of the tenancy, the guarantor (where his liability to do so is not wholly discharged by any such variation of the tenant covenants of the tenancy) shall not be liable under the agreement to pay any amount in respect of the covenant to the extent that the amount is referable to any such variation.

(4) For the purposes of this section a variation of the tenant covenants of a tenancy is a 'relevant variation' if either—

(a)   the landlord has, at the time of the variation, an absolute right to refuse to allow it; or

(b)   the landlord would have had such a right if the variation had been sought by the former tenant immediately before the assignment by him but, between the time of that assignment and the time of the variation, the tenant covenants of the tenancy have been so varied as to deprive the landlord of such a right.

(5) In determining whether the landlord has or would have had such a right at any particular time regard shall be had to all the circumstances (including the effect of any provision made by or under any enactment).

(6) Nothing in this section applies to any variation of the tenant covenants of a tenancy effected before the date on which this Act comes into force.

(7) In this section 'variation' means a variation whether effected by deed or otherwise.

Overriding leases

19.   Right of former tenant or his guarantor to overriding lease

(1)   Where in respect of any tenancy ('the relevant tenancy') any person ('the claimant') makes full payment of an amount which he has been duly required to pay in accordance with section 17, together with any interest payable, he shall be entitled (subject to and in accordance with this section) to have the landlord under that tenancy grant him an overriding lease of the premises demised by the tenancy.

(2)   For the purposes of this section 'overriding lease' means a tenancy of the reversion expectant on the relevant tenancy which—

(a)   is granted for a term equal to the remainder of the term of the relevant tenancy plus three days or the longest period (less than three days) that will not wholly displace the landlord's reversionary interest expectant on the relevant tenancy, as the case may require; and

(b)   (subject to subsections (3) and (4) and to any modifications agreed to by the claimant and the landlord) otherwise contains the same covenants as the relevant tenancy, as they have effect immediately before the grant of the lease.

(3)   An overriding lease shall not be required to reproduce any covenant of the relevant tenancy to the extent that the covenant is (in whatever terms) expressed to be a personal covenant between the landlord and the tenant under that tenancy.

(4)   If any right, liability or other matter arising under a covenant of the relevant tenancy falls to be determined or otherwise operates (whether expressly or otherwise) by reference to the commencement of that tenancy—

(a)   the corresponding covenant of the overriding lease shall be so framed that that right, liability or matter falls to be determined or otherwise operates by reference to the commencement of that tenancy; but

(b)   the overriding lease shall not be required to reproduce any covenant of that tenancy to the extent that it has become spent by the time that that lease is granted.

(5)   A claim to exercise the right to an overriding lease under this section is made by the claimant making a request for such a lease to the landlord; and any such request—

(a)   must be made to the landlord in writing and specify the payment by virtue of which the claimant claims to be entitled to the lease ('the qualifying payment'); and

(b)   must be so made at the time of making the qualifying payment or within the period of 12 months beginning with the date of that payment.

(6)   Where the claimant duly makes such a request—

(a)   the landlord shall (subject to subsection (7)) grant and deliver to the claimant an overriding lease of the demised premises within a reasonable time of the request being received by the landlord; and

(b)   the claimant—

(i)   shall thereupon deliver to the landlord a counterpart of the lease duly executed by the claimant, and

(ii)   shall be liable for the landlord's reasonable costs of and incidental to the grant of the lease.

(7)   The landlord shall not be under any obligation to grant an overriding lease of the demised premises under this section at a time when the relevant tenancy has been determined; and a claimant shall not be entitled to the grant of such a lease if at the time when he makes his request—

(a)   the landlord has already granted such a lease and that lease remains in force; or

(b)   another person has already duly made a request for such a lease to the landlord and that request has been neither withdrawn nor abandoned by that person.

(8)   Where two or more requests are duly made on the same day, then for the purposes of subsection (7)—

(a)   a request made by a person who was liable for the qualifying payment as a former tenant shall be treated as made before a request made by a person who was so liable as a guarantor; and

(b)   a request made by a person whose liability in respect of the covenant in question commenced earlier than any such liability of another person shall be treated as made before a request made by that other person.

(9)   Where a claimant who has duly made a request for an overriding lease under this section subsequently withdraws or abandons the request before he is granted such a lease by the landlord, the claimant shall be liable for the landlord's reasonable costs incurred in pursuance of the request down to the time of its withdrawal or abandonment; and for the purposes of this section—

(a)   a claimant's request is withdrawn by the claimant notifying the landlord in writing that he is withdrawing his request; and

(b)   a claimant is to be regarded as having abandoned his request if—

(i)   the landlord has requested the claimant in writing to take, within such reasonable period as is specified in the landlord's request, all or any of the remaining steps required to be taken by the claimant before the lease can be granted, and

(ii)   the claimant fails to comply with the landlord's request, and is accordingly to be regarded as having abandoned it at the time when that period expires.

(10)   Any request or notification under this section may be sent by post.

(11)   The preceding provisions of this section shall apply where the landlord is the tenant under an overriding lease granted under this section as they apply where no such lease has been granted; and accordingly there may be two or more such leases interposed between the first such lease and the relevant tenancy.

20.   Overriding leases: supplementary provisions

(1)   For the purposes of section 1 an overriding lease shall be a new tenancy only if the relevant tenancy is a new tenancy.

(2)   Every overriding lease shall state—

(a)   that it is a lease granted under section 19, and

(b)   whether it is or is not a new tenancy for the purposes of section 1; and any such statement shall comply with such requirements as may be prescribed by rules made in pursuance of section 144 of the Land Registration Act 1925 (power to make general rules).

(3)   A claim that the landlord has failed to comply with subsection (6)(a) of section 19 may be made the subject of civil proceedings in like manner as any other claim in tort for breach of statutory duty; and if the claimant

under that section fails to comply with subsection (6)(b)(i) of that section he shall not be entitled to exercise any of the rights otherwise exercisable by him under the overriding lease.

(4) An overriding lease—

(a) shall be deemed to be authorised as against the persons interested in any mortgage of the landlord's interest (however created or arising); and

(b) shall be binding on any such persons;

and if any such person is by virtue of such a mortgage entitled to possession of the documents of title relating to the landlord's interest—

(i) the landlord shall within one month of the execution of the lease deliver to that person the counterpart executed in pursuance of section 19(6)(b)(i); and

(ii) if he fails to do so, the instrument creating or evidencing the mortgage shall apply as if the obligation to deliver a counterpart were included in the terms of the mortgage as set out in that instrument.

(5) It is hereby declared—

(a) that the fact that an overriding lease takes effect subject to the relevant tenancy shall not constitute a breach of any covenant of the lease against subletting or parting with possession of the premises demised by the lease or any part of them; and

(b) that each of sections 16, 17 and 18 applies where the tenancy referred to in subsection (1) of that section is an overriding lease as it applies in other cases falling within that subsection.

(6) No tenancy shall be registrable under the Land Charges Act 1972 or be taken to be an estate contract within the meaning of that Act by reason of any right or obligation that may arise under section 19, and any right arising from a request made under that section shall not be an overriding interest within the meaning of the Land Registration Act 1925; but any such request shall be registrable under the Land Charges Act 1972, or may be the subject of a notice or caution under the Land Registration Act 1925, as if it were an estate contract.

(7) In this section—

(a) 'mortgage' includes 'charge'; and

(b) any expression which is also used in section 19 has the same meaning as in that section.

Forfeiture and disclaimer

21. Forfeiture or disclaimer limited to part only of demised premises

(1) Where—

(a) as a result of one or more assignments a person is the tenant of part only of the premises demised by a tenancy, and

(b)   under a proviso or stipulation in the tenancy there is a right of re-entry or forfeiture for a breach of a tenant covenant of the tenancy, and

(c)   the right is (apart from this subsection) exercisable in relation to that part and other land demised by the tenancy,

the right shall nevertheless, in connection with a breach of any such covenant by that person, be taken to be a right exercisable only in relation to that part.

(2)   Where—

(a)   a company which is being wound up, or a trustee in bankruptcy, is as a result of one or more assignments the tenant of part only of the premises demised by a tenancy, and

(b)   the liquidator of the company exercises his power under section 178 of the Insolvency Act 1986, or the trustee in bankruptcy exercises his power under section 315 of that Act, to disclaim property demised by the tenancy, the power is exercisable only in relation to the part of the premises referred to in paragraph (a).

Landlord's consent to assignments

22.   Imposition of conditions regulating giving of landlord's consent to assignments

After subsection (1) of section 19 of the Landlord and Tenant Act 1927 (provisions as to covenants not to assign etc. without licence or consent) there shall be inserted—

'(1A)   Where the landlord and the tenant under a qualifying lease have entered into an agreement specifying for the purposes of this subsection—

(a)   any circumstances in which the landlord may withhold his licence or consent to an assignment of the demised premises or any part of them, or

(b)   any conditions subject to which any such licence or consent may be granted,

then the landlord—

(i)   shall not be regarded as unreasonably withholding his licence or consent to any such assignment if he withholds it on the ground (and it is the case) that any such circumstances exist, and

(ii)   if he gives any such licence or consent subject to any such conditions, shall not be regarded as giving it subject to unreasonable conditions;

and section 1 of the Landlord and Tenant Act 1988 (qualified duty to consent to assignment etc.) shall have effect subject to the provisions of this subsection.

(1B)   Subsection (1A) of this section applies to such an agreement as is mentioned in that subsection—

(a)   whether it is contained in the lease or not, and

(b)   whether it is made at the time when the lease is granted or at any other time falling before the application for the landlord's licence or consent is made.

(1C)   Subsection (1A) shall not, however, apply to any such agreement to the extent that any circumstances or conditions specified in it are framed by reference to any matter falling to be determined by the landlord or by any other person for the purposes of the agreement, unless under the terms of the agreement—

(a)   that person's power to determine that matter is required to be exercised reasonably, or

(b)   the tenant is given an unrestricted right to have any such determination reviewed by a person independent of both landlord and tenant whose identity is ascertainable by reference to the agreement, and in the latter case the agreement provides for the determination made by any such independent person on the review to be conclusive as to the matter in question.

(1D)   In its application to a qualifying lease, subsection (1)(b) of this section shall not have effect in relation to any assignment of the lease.

(1E)   In subsections (1A) and (1D) of this section—

(a)   "qualifying lease" means any leasee which is a new tenancy for the purposes of section 1 of the Landlord and Tenant (Covenants) Act 1995 other than a residential lease, namely a lease by which a building or part of a building is let wholly or mainly as a single private residence; and

(b)   references to assignment include parting with possession on assignment.'

Supplemental

23.   Effects of becoming subject to liability under, or entitled to benefit of, covenant etc.

(1)   Where as a result of an assignment a person becomes by virtue of this Act, bound by or entitled to the benefit of a covenant, he shall not by virtue of this Act have any liability or rights under the covenant in relation to any time falling before the assignment.

(2)   Subsection (1) does not preclude any such rights being expressly assigned to the person in question.

(3)   Where as a result of an assignment a person becomes, by virtue of this Act, entitled to a right of re-entry contained in a tenancy, that right shall be exercisable in relation to any breach of a covenant of the tenancy occurring before the assignment as in relation to one occurring thereafter,

unless by reason of any waiver or release it was not so exercisable immediately before the assignment.

24. Effects of release from liability under, or loss of benefit of, covenant

(1) Any release of a person from a covenant by virtue of this Act does not affect any liability of his arising from a breach of the covenant occurring before the release.

(2) Where—

(a) by virtue of this Act a tenant is released from a tenant covenant of a tenancy, and

(b) immediately before the release another person is bound by a covenant of the tenancy imposing any liability or penalty in the event of a failure to comply with that tenant covenant,

then, as from the release of the tenant, that other person is released from the covenant mentioned in paragraph (b) to the same extent as the tenant is released from that tenant covenant.

(3) Where a person bound by a landlord or tenant covenant of a tenancy—

(a) assigns the whole or part of his interest in the premises demised by the tenancy, but

(b) is not released by virtue of this Act from the covenant (with the result that subsection (1) does not apply),

the assignment does not affect any liability of his arising from a breach of the covenant occurring before the assignment.

(4) Where by virtue of this Act a person ceases to be entitled to the benefit of a covenant, this does not affect any rights of his arising from a breach of the covenant occurring before he ceases to be so entitled.

25. Agreement void if it restricts operation of the Act

(1) Any agreement relating to a tenancy is void to the extent that—

(a) it would apart from this section have effect to exclude, modify or otherwise frustrate the operation of any provision of this Act, or

(b) it provides for—

(i) the termination or surrender of the tenancy, or

(ii) the imposition on the tenant of any penalty, disability or liability,

in the event of the operation of any provision of this Act, or

(c) it provides for any of the matters referred to in paragraph (b)(i) or (ii) and does so (whether expressly or otherwise) in connection with, or in consequence of, the operation of any provision of this Act.

(2) To the extent that an agreement relating to a tenancy constitutes a covenant (whether absolute or qualified) against the assignment, or parting

with the possession, of the premises demised by the tenancy or any part of them—

(a) the agreement is not void by virtue of subsection (1) by reason only of the fact that as such the covenant prohibits or restricts any such assignment or parting with possession; but

(b) paragraph (a) above does not otherwise affect the operation of that subsection in relation to the agreement (and in particular does not preclude its application to the agreement to the extent that it purports to regulate the giving of, or the making of any application for, consent to any such assignment or parting with possession).

(3) In accordance with section 16(1) nothing in this section applies to any agreement to the extent that it is an authorised guarantee agreement; but (without prejudice to the generality of subsection (1) above) an agreement is void to the extent that it is one falling within section 16(4)(a) or (b).

(4) This section applies to an agreement relating to a tenancy whether or not the agreement is—

(a) contained in the instrument creating the tenancy; or

(b) made before the creation of the tenancy.

26. Miscellaneous savings etc.

(1) Nothing in this Act is to be read as preventing—

(a) a party to a tenancy from releasing a person from a landlord covenant or a tenant covenant of the tenancy; or

(b) the parties to a tenancy from agreeing to an apportionment of liability under such a covenant.

(2) Nothing in this Act affects the operation of section 3(3A) of the Landlord and Tenant Act 1985 (preservation of former landlord's liability until tenant notified of new landlord).

(3) No apportionment which has become binding in accordance with section 10 shall be affected by any order or decision made under or by virtue of any enactment not contained in this Act which relates to apportionment.

27. Notices for the purposes of the Act

(1) The form of any notice to be served for the purposes of section 8, 10 or 17 shall be prescribed by regulations made by the Lord Chancellor by statutory instrument.

(2) The regulations shall require any notice served for the purposes of section 8(1) or 10(1) ('the initial notice') to include—

(a) an explanation of the significance of the notice and the options available to the person on whom it is served;

(b) a statement that any objections to the proposed release, or (as the case may be) to the proposed effect of the apportionment, must be made by notice in writing served on the person or persons by whom the initial notice is served within the period of four weeks beginning with the day on which the initial notice is served; and

(c)   an address in England and Wales to which any such objections may be sent.

(3)   The regulations shall require any notice served for the purposes of section 17 to include an explanation of the significance of the notice.

(4)   If any notice purporting to be served for the purposes of section 8(1), 10(1) or 17 is not in the prescribed form, or in a form substantially to the same effect, the notice shall not be effective for the purposes of section 8, section 10 or section 17 (as the case may be).

(5)   Section 23 of the Landlord and Tenant Act 1927 shall apply in relation to the service of notices for the purposes of section 8, 10 or 17.

(6)   Any statutory instrument made under this section shall be subject to annulment in pursuance of a resolution of either House of Parliament.

28. Interpretation

(1)   In this Act (unless the context otherwise requires)—

'assignment' includes equitable assignment and in addition (subject to section 11) assignment in breach of a covenant of a tenancy or by operation of law;

'authorised guarantee agreement' means an agreement which is an authorised guarantee agreement for the purposes of section 16;

'collateral agreement', in relation to a tenancy, means any agreement collateral to the tenancy, whether made before or after its creation;

'consent' includes licence;

'covenant' includes term, condition and obligation, and references to a covenant (or any description of covenant) of a tenancy include a covenant (or a covenant of that description) contained in a collateral agreement;

'landlord' and 'tenant', in relation to a tenancy, mean the person for the time being entitled to the reversion expectant on the term of the tenancy and the person so entitled to that term respectively;

'landlord covenant', in relation to a tenancy, means a covenant falling to be complied with by the landlord of premises demised by the tenancy;

'new tenancy' means a tenancy which is a new tenancy for the purposes of section 1;

'reversion' means the interest expectant on the termination of a tenancy;

'tenancy' means any lease or other tenancy and includes—

(a)   a sub-tenancy, and

(b)   an agreement for a tenancy,

but does not include a mortgage term;

'tenant covenant', in relation to a tenancy, means a covenant falling to be complied with by the tenant of premises demised by the tenancy.

(2) For the purposes of any reference in this Act to a covenant falling to be complied with in relation to a particular part of the premises demised by a tenancy, a covenant falls to be so complied with if—

(a) it in terms applies to that part of the premises, or

(b) in its practical application it can be attributed to that part of the premises (whether or not it can also be so attributed to other individual parts of those premises).

(3) Subsection (2) does not apply in relation to covenants to pay money; and, for the purposes of any reference in this Act to a covenant falling to be complied with in relation to a particular part of the premises demised by a tenancy, a covenant of a tenancy which is a covenant to pay money falls to be so complied with if—

(a) the covenant in terms applies to that part; or

(b) the amount of the payment is determinable specifically by reference—

(i) to that part, or

(ii) to anything falling to be done by or for a person as tenant or occupier of that part (if it is a tenant covenant), or

(iii) to anything falling to be done by or for a person as landlord of that part (if it is a landlord covenant).

(4) Where two or more persons jointly constitute either the landlord or the tenant in relation to a tenancy, any reference in this Act to the landlord or the tenant is a reference to both or all of the persons who jointly constitute the landlord or the tenant, as the case may be (and accordingly nothing in section 13 applies in relation to the rights and liabilities of such persons between themselves).

(5) References in this Act to the assignment by a landlord of the reversion in the whole or part of the premises demised by a tenancy are to the assignment by him of the whole of his interest (as owner of the reversion) in the whole or part of those premises.

(6) For the purposes of this Act—

(a) any assignment (however effected) consisting in the transfer of the whole of the landlord's interest (as owner of the reversion) in any premises demised by a tenancy shall be treated as an assignment by the landlord of the reversion in those premises even if it is not effected by him; and

(b) any assignment (however effected) consisting in the transfer of the whole of the tenant's interest in any premises demised by a tenancy shall be treated as an assignment by the tenant of those premises even if it is not effected by him.

29. Crown application

This Act binds the Crown.

30. Consequential amendments and repeals

(1)　The enactments specified in Schedule 1 are amended in accordance with that Schedule, the amendments being consequential on the provisions of this Act.

(2)　The enactments specified in Schedule 2 are repealed to the extent specified.

(3)　Subsections (1) and (2) do not affect the operation of—

　　(a)　section 77 of, or Part IX or X of Schedule 2 to, the Law of Property Act 1925, or

　　(b)　section 24(1)(b) or (2) of the Land Registration Act 1925,

in relation to tenancies which are not new tenancies.

(4)　In consequence of this Act nothing in the following provisions, namely—

　　(a)　sections 78 and 79 of the Law of the Property Act 1925 (benefit and burden of covenants relating to land), and

　　(b)　sections 141 and 142 of that Act (running of benefit and burden of covenants with reversion),

shall apply in relation to new tenancies.

(5)　The Lord Chancellor may by order made by statutory instrument make, in the case of such enactments as may be specified in the order, such amendments or repeals in, or such modifications of, those enactments as appear to him to be necessary or expedient in consequence of any provision of this Act.

(6)　Any statutory instrument made under subsection (5) shall be subject to annulment in pursuance of a resolution of either House of Parliament.

31. Commencement

(1)　The provisions of this Act come into force on such day as the Lord Chancellor may appoint by order made by statutory instrument.

(2)　An order under this section may contain such transitional provisions and savings (whether or not involving the modification of any enactment) as appear to the Lord Chancellor necessary or expedient in connection with the provisions brought into force by the order.

32. Short title and extent

(1)　This Act may be cited as the Landlord and Tenant (Covenants) Act 1995.

(2)　This Act extends to England and Wales only.

SCHEDULES

Section 30(1)   SCHEDULE 1
                    CONSEQUENTIAL AMENDMENTS

Trustee Act 1925 (c. 19)

1. In section 26 of the Trustee Act 1925 (protection against liability in
respect of rents and covenants), after subsection (1) insert—

'(1A) Where a personal representative or trustee has as such entered
into, or may as such be required to enter into, an authorised guarantee
agreement with respect to any lease comprised in the estate of a deceased
testator or intestate or a trust estate (and, in a case where he has entered
into such an agreement, he has satisfied all liabilities under it which may
have accrued and been claimed up to the date of distribution)—

(a) he may distribute the residuary real and personal estate of the
deceased testator or intestate, or the trust estate, to or amongst the persons
entitled thereto—

(i) without appropriating any part of the estate of the deceased,
or the trust estate, to meet any future liability (or, as the case may be, any
liability) under any such agreement, and

(ii) notwithstanding any potential liability of his to enter into any
such agreement; and

(b) notwithstanding such distribution, he shall not be personally
liable in respect of any subsequent claim (or, as the case may be, any
claim) under any such agreement.

In this subsection "authorised guarantee agreement" has the same
meaning as in the Landlord and Tenant (Covenants) Act 1995.'

Law of Property Act 1925 (c.20)

2. In section 77 of the Law of Property Act 1925 (implied covenants in
conveyances subject to rents), for subsection (2) substitute—

'(2) Where in a conveyance for valuable consideration, other than a
mortgage, part of land affected by a rentcharge is, without the consent
of the owner of the rentcharge, expressed to be conveyed subject to or
charged with the entire rent, paragraph (B)(i) of subsection (1) of this
section shall apply as if, in paragraph (i) of Part VIII of the Second
Schedule to this Act—

(a) any reference to the apportioned rent were to the entire rent;
and

(b) the words "(other than the covenant to pay the entire rent)"
were omitted.

(2A) Where in a conveyance for valuable consideration, other than a mortgage, part of land affected by a rentcharge is, without the consent of the owner of the rentcharge, expressed to be conveyed, discharged or exonerated from the entire rent, paragraph (B)(ii) of subsection (1) of this section shall apply as if, in paragraph (ii) of Part VIII of the Second Schedule to this Act—

(a) any reference to the balance of the rent were to the entire rent; and

(b) the words '', other than the covenant to pay the entire rent,'' were omitted.'

Landlord and Tenant Act 1954 (c. 56)

3. At the end of section 34 of the Landlord and Tenant Act 1954 (rent under new tenancy) insert—

'(4) It is hereby declared that the matters which are to be taken into account by the court in determining the rent include any effect on rent of the operation of the provisions of the Landlord and Tenant (Covenants) Act 1995.'

4.—(1) The existing provisions of section 35 of that Act (other terms of new tenancy) shall constitute subsection (1) of that section.

(2) After those provisions insert—

'(2) In subsection (1) of this section the reference to all relevant circumstances includes (without prejudice to the generality of that reference) a reference to the operation of the provisions of the Landlord and Tenant (Covenants) Act 1995.'

SCHEDULE 2

REPEALS

Chapter	Short title	Extent of repeal
15 & 16 Geo. 5 c. 20.	Law of Property Act 1925	In section 77, subsection (1)(C) and (D) and, in subsection (7), paragraph (c) and the 'or' preceding it. In Schedule 2, Parts IX and X.
15 & 16 Geo. 5 c. 21.	Land Registration Act 1925	Section 24(1)(b) and (2).

Appendix 2

Other Statutes

Law of Property Act 1925, sections 76-9, 140-4 and schedule 2

Covenants

76. Covenants for title

(1) In a conveyance there shall, in the several cases in this section mentioned, be deemed to be included, and there shall in those several cases, by virtue of this Act, be implied, a covenant to the effect in this section stated, by the person or by each person who conveys, as far as regards the subject-matter or share of subject-matter expressed to be conveyed by him, with the person, if one, to whom the conveyance is made, or with the persons jointly, if more than one, to whom the conveyance is made as joint tenants, or with each of the persons, if more than one, to whom the conveyance is (when the law permits) made as tenants in common, that is to say:

(A) In a conveyance for valuable consideration, other than a mortgage, a covenant by a person who conveys and is expressed to convey as beneficial owner in the terms set out in Part I. of the Second Schedule to this Act;

(B) In a conveyance of leasehold property for valuable consideration, other than a mortgage, a further covenant by a person who conveys and is expressed to convey as beneficial owner in the terms set out in Part II. of the Second Schedule to this Act;

(C) In a conveyance by way of mortgage (including a charge) a covenant by a person who conveys or charges and is expressed to convey or charge as beneficial owner in the terms set out in Part III. of the Second Schedule to this Act;

(D) In a conveyance by way of mortgage (including a charge) of freehold property subject to a rent or of leasehold property, a further covenant by a person who conveys or charges and is expressed to convey or charge as beneficial owner in the terms set out in Part IV. of the Second Schedule to this Act;

(E)   In a conveyance by way of settlement, a covenant by a person who conveys and is expressed to convey as settlor in the terms set out in Part V. of the Second Schedule to this Act;

(F)   In any conveyance, a covenant by every person who conveys and is expressed to convey as trustee or mortgagee, or as personal representative of a deceased person, or under an order of the court, in the terms set out in Part VI. of the Second Schedule to this Act, which covenant shall be deemed to extend to every such person's own acts only, and may be implied in an assent by a personal representative in like manner as in a conveyance by deed.

(2)   Where in a conveyance it is expressed that by direction of a person expressed to direct as beneficial owner another person conveys, then, for the purposes of this section, the person giving the direction, whether he conveys and is expressed to convey as beneficial owner or not, shall be deemed to convey and to be expressed to convey as beneficial owner the subject-matter so conveyed by his direction; and a covenant on his part shall be implied accordingly.

(3)   Where a wife conveys and is expressed to convey as beneficial owner, and the husband also conveys and is expressed to convey as beneficial owner, then, for the purposes of this section, the wife shall be deemed to convey and to be expressed to convey by direction of the husband, as beneficial owner; and, in addition to the covenant implied on the part of the wife, there shall also be implied, first, a covenant on the part of the husband as the person giving that direction, and secondly, a covenant on the part of the husband in the same terms as the covenant implied on the part of the wife.

(4)   Where in a conveyance a person conveying is not expressed to convey as beneficial owner, or as settlor, or as trustee, or as mortgagee, or as personal representative of a deceased person, or under an order of the court, or by direction of a person as beneficial owner, no covenant on the part of the person conveying shall be, by virtue of this section, implied in the conveyance.

(5)   In this section a conveyance does not include a demise by way of lease at a rent, but does include a charge and 'convey' has a corresponding meaning.

(6)   The benefit of a covenant implied as aforesaid shall be annexed and incident to, and shall go with, the estate or interest of the implied covenantee, and shall be capable of being enforced by every person in whom that estate or interest is, for the whole or any part thereof, from time to time vested.

(7)   A covenant implied as aforesaid may be varied or extended by a deed or an assent, and, as so varied or extended, shall, as far as may be, operate

in the like manner, and with all the like incidents, effects, and consequences, as if such variations or extensions were directed in this section to be implied.

(8) This section applies to conveyances made after the thirty-first day of December, eighteen hundred and eighty-one, but only to assents by a personal representative made after the commencement of this Act.

Note: See Law of Property (Miscellaneous Provisions) Act 1994, s. 10.

77. Implied covenants in conveyances subject to rents

(1) In addition to the covenants implied under Part I of the Law of Property (Miscellaneous Provisions) Act 1994, there shall in the several cases in this section mentioned, be deemed to be included and implied, a covenant to the effect in this section stated, by and with such persons as are hereinafter mentioned, that is to say:—

(A) In a conveyance for valuable consideration, other than a mortgage, of the entirety of the land affected by a rentcharge, a covenant by the grantee or joint and several covenants by the grantees, if more than one, with the conveying parties and with each of them, if more than one, in the terms set out in Part VII. of the Second Schedule to this Act. Where a rentcharge has been apportioned in respect of any land, with the consent of the owner of the rentcharge, the covenants in this paragraph shall be implied in the conveyance of that land in like manner as if the apportioned rentcharge were the rentcharge referred to, and the document creating the rentcharge related solely to that land:

(B) In a conveyance for valuable consideration, other than a mortgage, of part of land affected by a rentcharge, subject to a part of that rentcharge which has been or is by that conveyance apportioned (but in either case without the consent of the owner of the rentcharge) in respect of the land conveyed:—

(i) A covenant by the grantee of the land or joint and several covenants by the grantees, if more than one, with the conveying parties and with each of them, if more than one, in the terms set out in paragraph (i) of Part VIII. of the Second Schedule to this Act;

(ii) A covenant by a person who conveys or is expressed to convey as beneficial owner, or joint and several covenants by the persons who so convey or are expressed to so convey, if at the date of the conveyance any part of the land affected by such rentcharge is retained, with the grantees of the land and with each of them (if more than one) in the terms set out in paragraph (ii) of Part VIII. of the Second Schedule to this Act:

(C) In a conveyance for valuable consideration, other than a mortgage, of the entirety of the land comprised in a lease, for the residue of the term or interest created by the lease, a covenant by the assignee or joint and several covenants by the assignees (if more than one) with the conveying parties and with each of them (if more than one) in the terms set out in Part IX. of the Second Schedule to this Act. Where a rent has been apportioned in respect of any land, with the consent of the lessor, the covenants in this paragraph shall be implied in the conveyance of that land in like manner as if the apportioned rent were the original rent reserved, and the lease related solely to that land:

(D)   In a conveyance for valuable consideration, other than a mortgage, of part of the land comprised in a lease, for the residue of the term or interest created by the lease, subject to a part of the rent which has been or is by the conveyance apportioned (but in either case without the consent of the lessor) in respect of the land conveyed:—

(i)   A covenant by the assignee of the land, or joint and several covenants by the assignees, if more than one, with the conveying parties and with each of them, if more than one, in the terms set out in paragraph (i) of Part X. of the Second Schedule to this Act;

(ii)   A covenant by a person who conveys or is expressed to convey as beneficial owner, or joint and several covenants by the persons who so convey or are expressed to so convey, if at the date of the conveyance any part of the land comprised in the lease is retained, with the assignees of the land and with each of them (if more than one) in the terms set out in paragraph (ii) of Part X. of the Second Schedule to this Act.

(2)   Where in a conveyance for valuable consideration, other than a mortgage, part of land affected by a rentcharge is, without the consent of the owner of the rentcharge, expressed to be conveyed subject to or charged with the entire rent, paragraph (B)(i) of subsection (1) of this section shall apply as if, in paragraph (i) of Part VII. of the Second Schedule to this Act—

(a)   any reference to the apportioned rent were to the entire rent; and

(b)   the words '(other than the covenant to pay the entire rent)' were omitted.

(2A)   Where in a conveyance for valuable consideration, other than a mortgage, part of land affected by a rentcharge is, without the consent of the owner of the rentcharge, expressed to be conveyed discharged or exonerated from the entire rent, paragraph (B)(ii) of subsection (1) of this section shall apply as if, in paragraph (ii) of Part VIII of the Second Schedule to this Act—

(a)   any reference to the balance of the rent were to the entire rent; and

(b)   the words ', other than the covenant to pay the entire rent,' were omitted.

(3)   In this section 'conveyance' does not include a demise by way of lease at a rent.

(4)   Any convenant which would be implied under this section by reason of a person conveying or being expressed to convey as beneficial owner may, by express reference to this section, be implied, with or without variation, in a conveyance, whether or not for valuable consideration, by a person who conveys or is expressed to convey as settlor, or as trustee, or as mortgagee, or as personal representative of a deceased person, or under an order of the court.

(5)   The benefit of a covenant implied as aforesaid shall be annexed and incident to, and shall go with, the estate or interest of the implied covenantee, and shall be capable of being enforced by every person in whom that estate or interest is, for the whole or any part thereof, from time to time vested.

(6)   A covenant implied as aforesaid may be varied or extended by deed, and, as so varied or extended, shall, as far as may be, operate in the like manner, and with all the like incidents, effects and consequences, as if such variations or extensions were directed in this section to be implied.

(7)   In particular any covenant implied under this section may be extended by providing that—

(a)   the land conveyed; or

(b)   the part of the land affected by the rentcharge which remains vested in the covenantor; or

(c)   the part of the land demised which remains vested in the covenantor;

shall, as the case may require, stand charged with the payment of all money which may become payable under the implied covenant.

(8)   This section applies only to conveyances made after the commencement of this Act.

78.   Benefit of covenants relating to land

(1)   A covenant relating to any land of the covenantee shall be deemed to be made with the covenantee and his successors in title and the persons deriving title under him or them, and shall have effect as if such successors and other persons were expressed.

For the purposes of this subsection in connexion with covenants restrictive of the user of land 'successors in title' shall be deemed to include the owners and occupiers for the time being of the land of the covenantee intended to be benefited.

(2)   This section applies to covenants made after the commencement of this Act, but the repeal of section fifty-eight of the Conveyancing Act, 1881, does not affect the operation of covenants to which that section applied.

79. Burden of covenants relating to land

(1) A covenant relating to any land of a covenantor or capable of being bound by him, shall, unless a contrary intention is expressed, be deemed to be made by the covenantor on behalf of himself his successors in title and the persons deriving title under him or them, and, subject as aforesaid, shall have effect as if such successors and other persons were expressed.

This subsection extends to a covenant to do some act relating to the land, notwithstanding that the subject-matter may not be in existence when the covenant is made.

(2) For the purposes of this section in connexion with covenants restrictive of the user of land 'successors in title' shall be deemed to include the owners and occupiers for the time being of such land.

(3) This section applies only to covenants made after the commencement of this Act.

Note: Does not apply to tenancies created after the Landlord and Tenant (Covenants) Act 1995 comes into force.

140. Apportionment of conditions on severance

(1) Notwithstanding the severance by conveyance, surrender, or other-wise of the reversionary estate in any land comprised in a lease, and notwithstanding the avoidance or cesser in any other manner of the term granted by a lease as to part only of the land comprised therein, every condition or right of re-entry, and every other condition contained in the lease, shall be apportioned, and shall remain annexed to the severed parts of the reversionary estate as severed, and shall be in force with respect to the term whereon each severed part is reversionary, or the term in the part of the land as to which the term has not been surrendered, or has not been avoided or has not otherwise ceased, in like manner as if the land comprised in each severed part, or the land as to which the term remains subsisting, as the case may be, had alone originally been comprised in the lease.

(2) In this section 'right of re-entry' includes a right to determine the lease by notice to quit or otherwise; but where the notice is served by a person entitled to a severed part of the reversion so that it extends to part only of the land demised, the lessee may within one month determine the lease in regard to the rest of the land by giving to the owner of the reversionary estate therein a counter notice expiring at the same time as the original notice.

(3) This section applies to leases made before or after the commence-ment of this Act and whether the severance of the reversionary estate or the partial avoidance or cesser of the term was effected before or after such commencement:

Provided that, where the lease was made before the first day of January eighteen hundred and eighty-two nothing in this section shall affect the operation of a severance of the reversionary estate or partial avoidance or cesser of the term which was effected before the commencement of this Act.

141.   Rent and benefit of lessee's covenants to run with the reversion

(1)   Rent reserved by a lease, and the benefit of every covenant or provision therein contained, having reference to the subject-matter thereof, and on the lessee's part to be observed or performed, and every condition of re-entry and other condition therein contained, shall be annexed and incident to and shall go with the reversionary estate in the land, or in any part thereof, immediately expectant on the term granted by the lease, notwithstanding severance of that reversionary estate, and without prejudice to any liability affecting a covenantor or his estate.

(2)   Any such rent, covenant or provision shall be capable of being recovered, received, enforced, and taken advantage of, by the person from time to time entitled, subject to the term, to the income of the whole or any part, as the case may require, of the land leased.

(3)   Where that person becomes entitled by conveyance or otherwise, such rent, covenant or provision may be recovered, received, enforced or taken advantage of by him notwithstanding that he becomes so entitled after the condition of re-entry of forfeiture has become enforceable, but this subsection does not render enforceable any condition of re-entry or other condition waived or released before such person becomes entitled as aforesaid.

(4)   This section applies to leases made before or after the commencement of this Act, but does not affect the operation of—

(a)   any severance of the reversionary estate; or

(b)   any acquisition by conveyance or otherwise of the right to receive or enforce any rent covenant or provision;

effected before the commencement of this Act.

142.   Obligation of lessor's covenants to run with reversion

(1)   The obligation under a condition or of a covenant entered into by a lessor with reference to the subject-matter of the lease shall, if and as far as the lessor has power to bind the reversionary estate immediately expectant on the term granted by the lease, be annexed and incident to and shall go with that reversionary estate, or the several parts thereof, notwithstanding severance of that reversionary estate, and may be taken advantage of and enforced by the person in whom the term is from time to time vested by conveyance, devolution in law, or otherwise; and, if and as far as the lessor has power to bind the person from time to time entitled to that reversionary

estate, the obligation aforesaid may be taken advantage of and enforced against any person so entitled.

(2) This section applies to leases made before or after the commencement of this Act, whether the severance of the reversionary estate was effected before or after such commencement:

Provided that, where the lease was made before the first day of January eighteen hundred and eighty-two, nothing in this section shall affect the operation of any severance of the reversionary estate effected before such commencement.

This section takes effect without prejudice to any liability affecting a covenantor or his estate.

143. Effect of licences granted to lessees

(1) Where a licence is granted to a lessee to do any act, the licence, unless otherwise expressed, extends only—

(a) to the permission actually given; or

(b) to the specific breach of any provision or covenant referred to; or

(c) to any other matter thereby specifically authorised to be done; and the licence does not prevent any proceeding for any subsequent breach unless otherwise specified in the licence.

(2) Notwithstanding any such licence—

(a) All rights under covenants and powers of re-entry contained in the lease remain in full force and are available as against any subsequent breach of covenant, condition or other matter not specifically authorised or waived, in the same manner as if no licence had been granted; and

(b) The condition or right of entry remains in force in all respects as if the licence had not been granted, save in respect of the particular matter authorised to be done.

(3) Where in any lease there is a power or condition of re-entry on the lessee assigning, subletting or doing any other specified act without a licence, and a licence is granted—

(a) to any one or two or more lessees to do any act, or to deal with his equitable share or interest; or

(b) to any lessee, or to any one of two or more lessees to assign or underlet part only of the property, or to do any act in respect of part only of the property; the licence does not operate to extinguish the right of entry in case of any breach of covenant or condition by the co-lessees of the other shares or interests in the property, or by the lessee or lessees of the rest of the property (as the case may be) in respect of such shares or interests or remaining property, but the right of entry remains in force in respect of the shares, interests or property not the subject of the licence.

This subsection does not authorise the grant after the commencement of this Act of a licence to create an undivided share in a legal estate.

(4)   This section applies to licences granted after the thirteenth day of August, eighteen hundred and fifty-nine.

144.   No fine to be exacted for licence to assign

In all leases containing a covenant, condition, or agreement against assigning, underletting, or parting with the possession, or disposing of the land or property leased without licence or consent, such covenant, condition, or agreement shall, unless the lease contains an express provision to the contrary, be deemed to be subject to a proviso to the effect that no fine or sum of money in the nature of a fine shall be payable for or in respect of such licence or consent; but this proviso does not preclude the right to require the payment of a reasonable sum in respect of any legal or other expense incurred in relation to such licence or consent.

SCHEDULE 2   IMPLIED COVENANTS

PART I   COVENANT IMPLIED IN A CONVEYANCE FOR VALUABLE CONSIDERATION, OTHER THAN A MORTGAGE, BY A PERSON WHO CONVEYS AND IS EXPRESSED TO CONVEY AS BENEFICIAL OWNER

That, notwithstanding anything by the person who so conveys or any one through whom he derives title. otherwise than by purchase for value, made, done, executed, or omitted, or knowingly suffered, the person who so conveys has, with the concurrence of every other person, if any, conveying by his direction, full power to convey the subject-matter expressed to be conveyed, subject as, if so expressed, and in the manner in which, it is expressed to be conveyed, and that, notwithstanding anything as aforesaid, that subject-matter shall remain to and be quietly entered upon, received, and held, occupied, enjoyed, and taken, by the person to whom the conveyance is expressed to be made, and any person deriving title under him, and the benefit thereof shall be received and taken accordingly, without any lawful interruption or disturbance by the person who so conveys or any person conveying by his direction, or rightfully claiming or to claim by, through, under, or in trust for the person who so conveys, or any person conveying by his direction, or by, through, or under any one (not being a person claiming in respect of an estate or interest subject whereto the conveyance is expressly made), through whom the person who so conveys derives title, otherwise than by purchase for value:

And that, freed and discharged from, or otherwise by the person who so conveys sufficiently indemnified against, all such estates, incumbrances, claims and demands, other than those subject to which the conveyance is expressly made, as, either before or after the date of the conveyance, have been or shall be made, occasioned, or suffered by that person or by any person conveying by his direction, or by any person rightfully claiming by, through, under, or in trust for the person who so conveys, or by, through, or under any person conveying by his direction, by, through, or under any one through whom the person who so conveys derives title, otherwise than by purchase for value.

And further, that the person who so conveys, and any person conveying by his direction, and every other person having or rightfully claiming any estate or interest in the subject-matter of conveyance, other than an estate or interest subject whereto the conveyance is expressly made, by, through, under, or in trust for the person who so conveys, or by, through, or under any person conveying by his direction, or by, through, or under any one through whom the person who so conveys derives title, otherwise than by purchase for value, will from time to time and at all times after the date of the conveyance, on the request and at the cost of any person to whom the conveyance is expressed to be made, or of any person deriving title under him, execute and do all such lawful assurances and things for further or more perfectly assuring the subject-matter of the conveyance to the person to whom the conveyance is made, and to those deriving title under him, subject as, if so expressed, and in the manner in which the conveyance is expressed to be made, as by him or them or any of them shall be reasonably required.

In the above covenant a purchase for value shall not be deemed to include a conveyance in consideration of marriage.

PART II   FURTHER COVENANT IMPLIED IN A CONVEYANCE OF LEASEHOLD PROPERTY FOR VALUABLE CONSIDERATION, OTHER THAN A MORTGAGE, BY A PERSON WHO CONVEYS AND IS EXPRESSED TO CONVEY AS BENEFICIAL OWNER

That, notwithstanding anything by the person who so conveys, or any one through whom he derives title, otherwise than by purchase for value, made, done, executed, or omitted, or knowingly suffered, the lease or grant creating the term or estate for which the land is conveyed is, at the time of conveyance, a good, valid, and effectual lease or grant of the property conveyed, and is in full force, unforfeited, unsurrendered, and has in nowise become void or voidable, and that, notwithstanding anything as aforesaid, all the rents reserved by, and all the covenants, conditions, and agreements contained in, the lease or grant, and on the part of the lessee or grantee and the persons deriving title under him to be paid, observed, and performed, have been paid, observed, and performed up to the time of conveyance.

In the above covenant a purchase for value shall not be deemed to include a conveyance in consideration of marriage.

PART III   COVENANT IMPLIED IN A CONVEYANCE BY WAY OF MORTGAGE BY A PERSON WHO CONVEYS AND IS EXPRESSED TO CONVEY AS BENEFICIAL OWNER

That the person who so conveys, has, with the concurrence of every other person, if any, conveying by his direction, full power to convey the subject-matter expressed to be conveyed by him, subject as, if so expressed, and in the manner in which it is expressed to be conveyed:

And also that, if default is made in payment of the money intended to be secured by the conveyance, or any interest thereon, or any part of that money or interest, contrary to any provision in the conveyance, it shall be lawful for the person to whom the conveyance is expressed to be made, and the persons deriving title under him, to enter into and upon, or receive, and thenceforth quietly hold, occupy, and enjoy or take and have, the subject-matter expressed to be conveyed, or any part thereof, without any lawful interruption or disturbance by the person who so conveys, or any person conveying by his direction, or any other person (not being a person claiming in respect of an estate or interest subject whereto the conveyance is expressly made):

And that, freed and discharged from, or otherwise by the person who so conveys sufficiently indemnified against all estates, incumbrances, claims, and demands whatever, other than those subject whereto the conveyance is expressly made:

And further, that the person who so conveys and every person conveying by his direction, and every person deriving title under any of them, and every other person having or rightfully claiming any estate or interest in the subject-matter of conveyance, or any part thereof, other than an estate or interest subject whereto the conveyance is expressly made, will from time to time and at all times, on the request of any person to whom the conveyance is expressed to be made, or of any person deriving title under him, but, as long as any right of redemption exists under the conveyance, at the cost of the person so conveying, or of those deriving title under him, and afterwards at the cost of the person making the request, execute and do all such lawful assurances and things for further or more perfectly assuring the subject-matter of conveyance and every part thereof to the person to whom the conveyance is made, and to those deriving title under him, subject as, if so expressed, and in the manner in which the conveyance is expressed to be made, as by him or them or any of them shall be reasonably required.

The above covenant in the case of a charge shall have effect as if for references to 'conveys', 'conveyed' and 'conveyance' there were substituted respectively references to 'charges', charged' and 'charge'.

PART IV   COVENANT IMPLIED IN A CONVEYANCE BY WAY OF MORTGAGE OF FREEHOLD PROPERTY SUBJECT TO A RENT OR OF LEASEHOLD PROPERTY BY A PERSON WHO CONVEYS AND IS EXPRESSED TO CONVEY AS BENEFICIAL OWNER

That the lease or grant creating the term or estate for which the land is held is, at the time of conveyance, a good, valid, and effectual lease or grant of the land conveyed and is in full force, unforfeited, and unsurrendered and has in nowise become void or voidable, and that all the rents reserved by, and all the covenants, conditions, and agreements contained in, the lease or grant, and on the part of the lessee or grantee and the persons deriving title under him to be paid, observed, and performed, have been paid, observed, and performed up to the time of conveyance:

And also that the person so conveying, or the persons deriving title under him, will at all times, as long as any money remains owing on the security of the conveyance, pay, observe, and perform, or cause to be paid, observed, and performed all the rents reserved by, and all the covenants, conditions, and agreements contained in, the lease or grant, and on the part of the lessee or grantee and the persons deriving title under him to be paid, observed, and performed, and will keep the person to whom the conveyance is made, and those deriving title under him, indemnified against all actions, proceedings, costs, charges, damages, claims and demands, if any, to be incurred or sustained by him or them by reason of the non-payment of such rent or the non-observance or non-performance of such covenants, conditions, and agreements, or any of them.

The above covenant in the case of a charge shall have effect as if for references to 'conveys', 'conveyed' and 'conveyance' there were substituted respectively references to 'charges', charged' and 'charge'.

PART V   COVENANT IMPLIED IN A CONVEYANCE BY WAY OF SETTLEMENT, BY A PERSON WHO CONVEYS AND IS EXPRESSED TO CONVEY AS SETTLOR

That the person so conveying, and every person deriving title under him by deed or act or operation of law in his lifetime subsequent to that conveyance, or by testamentary disposition or devolution in law, on his death, will, from time to time, and at all times, after the date of that conveyance, at the request and cost of any person deriving title thereunder, execute and do all such lawful assurances and things for further or more perfectly assuring the subject-matter of the conveyance to the persons to whom the conveyance is made and those deriving title under them, as by them or any of them shall be reasonably required, subject as, if so expressed, and in the manner in which the conveyance is expressed to be made.

PART VI   COVENANT IMPLIED IN ANY CONVEYANCE, BY EVERY PERSON WHO CONVEYS AND IS EXPRESSED TO CONVEY AS TRUSTEE OR MORTGAGEE, OR AS PERSONAL REPRESENTATIVE OF A DECEASED PERSON, OR UNDER AN ORDER OF THE COURT

That the person so conveying has not executed or done, or knowingly suffered, or been party or privy to, any deed or thing, whereby or by means whereof the subject-matter of the conveyance, or any part thereof, is or may be impeached, charged, affected, or incumbered in title, estate, or otherwise, or whereby or by means whereof the person who so conveys is in anywise hindered from conveying the subject-matter of the conveyance, or any part thereof, in the manner in which it is expressed to be conveyed.

The foregoing covenant may be implied in an assent in like manner as in a conveyance by deed.

PART VII   COVENANT IMPLIED IN A CONVEYANCE FOR VALUABLE CONSIDERATION, OTHER THAN A MORTGAGE, OF THE ENTIRETY OF LAND AFFECTED BY A RENTCHARGE

That the grantees or the persons deriving title under them will at all times, from the date of the conveyance or other date therein stated, duly pay the said rentcharge and observe and perform all the covenants, agreements and conditions contained in the deed or other document creating the rentcharge, and thenceforth on the part of the owner of the land to be observed and performed:

And also will at all times, from the date aforesaid, save harmless and keep indemnified the conveying parties and their respective estates and effects, from and against all proceedings, costs, claims and expenses on account of any omission to pay the said rentcharge or any part thereof, or any breach of any of the said covenants, agreements and conditions.

PART VIII   COVENANTS IMPLIED IN A CONVEYANCE FOR VALUABLE CONSIDERATION, OTHER THAN A MORTGAGE, OF PART OF LAND AFFECTED BY A RENTCHARGE, SUBJECT TO A PART (NOT LEGALLY APPORTIONED) OF THAT RENTCHARGE

(i)   That the grantees, or the persons deriving title under them, will at all times, from the date of the conveyance or other date therein stated, pay the apportioned rent and observe and perform all the covenants (other than the covenant to pay the entire rent) and conditions contained in the deed or other document creating the rentcharge, so far as the same relate to the land conveyed:

And also will at all times, from the date aforesaid, save harmless and keep indemnified the conveying parties and their respective estates and effects, from and against all proceedings, cost, claims and expenses on account of any omission to pay the said apportioned rent, or any breach of any of the said covenants and conditions, so far as the same relate as aforesaid.

(ii)   That the conveying parties, or the persons deriving title under them, will at all times, from the date of the conveyance or other date therein stated, pay the balance of the rentcharge (after deducting the apportioned rent aforesaid, and any other rents similarly apportioned in respect of land not retained), and observe and perform all the covenants, other than the covenant to pay the entire rent, and conditions contained in the deed or other document creating the rentcharge, so far as the same relate to the land not included in the conveyance and remaining vested in the covenantors:

And also will at times, from the date aforesaid, save harmless and keep indemnified the grantees and their estates and effects, from and against all proceedings, costs, claims and expenses on account of any omission to pay the aforesaid balance of the rentcharge, or any breach of any of the said covenants and conditions so far as they relate as aforesaid.

PART IX COVENANT IN A CONVEYANCE FOR VALUABLE CONSIDERATION, OTHER THAN A MORTGAGE, OF THE ENTIRETY OF THE LAND COMPRISED IN A LEASE FOR THE RESIDUE OF THE TERM OR INTEREST CREATED BY THE LEASE

That the assignees, or the persons deriving title under them, will at all times, from the date of the conveyance or other date therein stated, duly pay all rent becoming due under the lease creating the term or interest for which the land is conveyed, and observe and perform all the covenants, agreements and conditions therein contained and thenceforth on the part of the lessees to be observed and performed:

And also will at all times, from the date aforesaid, save harmless and keep indemnified the conveying parties and their estates and effects, from and against any proceedings, costs, claims and expenses on account of any omission to pay the said rent or any breach of any of the said covenants, agreements and conditions.

PART X   COVENANT IMPLIED IN A CONVEYANCE FOR VALUABLE CONSIDERATION, OTHER THAN A MORTGAGE, OR PART OF THE LAND COMPRISED IN A LEASE, FOR THE RESIDUE OF THE TERM OR INTEREST CREATED BY THE LEASE, SUBJECT TO A PART (NOT LEGALLY APPORTIONED) OF THE RENT

(i)   That the assignees, or the persons deriving title under them, will at all times, from the date of the conveyance or other date therein stated, pay the apportioned rent and observe and perform all the covenants, other than the covenant to pay the entire rent, agreements and conditions contained in the lease creating the term or interest for which the land is conveyed, and thenceforth on the part of the lessees to be observed and performed, so far as the same relate to the land conveyed:

And also will at all times from the date aforesaid save harmless and keep indemnified, the conveying parties and their respective estates and effects, from and against all proceedings, costs, claims and expenses on account of any omission to pay the said apportioned rent or any breach of any of the said covenants, agreements and conditions so far as the same relate as aforesaid.

(ii)   That the conveying parties, or the persons deriving title under them, will at all times, from the date of the conveyance, or other date therein stated, pay the balance of the rent (after deducting the apportioned rent aforesaid and any other rents similarly apportioned in respect of land not retained) and observe and perform all the covenants, other than the covenant to pay the entire rent, agreements and conditions contained in the lease and on the part of the lessees to be observed and performed so far as the same relate to the land demised (other than the land comprised in the conveyance) and remaining vested in the covenantors:

And also will at all times, from the date aforesaid, save harmless and keep indemnified, the assignees and their estates and effects, from and against all proceedings, costs, claims and expenses on account of any omission to pay the aforesaid balance of the rent or any breach of any of the said covenants, agreements and conditions so far as they relate as aforesaid.

Landlord and Tenant Act 1927, sections 19, 20 and 23

19.   Provisions as to covenants not to assign, etc. without licence or consent.

(1)   In all leases whether made before or after the commencement of this Act containing a covenant condition or agreement against assigning, under-

letting, charging or parting with the possession of demised premises or any part thereof without licence or consent, such covenant condition or agreement shall, notwithstanding any express provision to the contrary, be deemed to be subject—

(a) to a proviso to the effect that such licence or consent is not to be unreasonably withheld, but this proviso does not preclude the right of the landlord to require payment of a reasonable sum in respect of any legal or other expenses incurred in connection with such licence or consent; and

(b) (if the lease is for more than forty years, and is made in consideration wholly or partially of the erection, or the substantial improvement, addition or alteration of buildings, and the lessor is not a Government department or local or public authority, or a statutory or public utility company) to a proviso to the effect that in the case of any assignment, under-letting, charging or parting with the possession (whether by the holders of the lease or any under-tenant whether immediate or not) effected more than seven years before the end of the term no consent or licence shall be required, if notice in writing of the transaction is given to the lessor within six months after the transaction is effected.

(1A) Where the landlord and the tenant under a qualifying lease have entered into an agreement specifying for the purposes of this subsection—

(a) any circumstances in which the landlord may withhold his licence or consent to an assignment of the demised premises of any part of them, or

(b) any conditions subject to which any such licence or consent may be granted,

then the landlord—

(i) shall not be regarded as unreasonably withholding his licence or consent to any such assignment if he withholds it on the ground (and it is the case) that any such circumstances exist, and

(ii) if he gives such licence or consent subject to any such conditions, shall not be regarded as giving it subject to unreasonable conditions;

and section 1 of the Landlord and Tenant Act 1988 (qualified duty to consent to assignment etc.) shall have effect subject to the provisions of this subsection.

(1B) Subsection (1A) of this section applies to such an agreement as is mentioned in that subsection—

(a) whether it is contained in the lease or not, and

(b) whether it is made at the time when the lease is granted or at any other time falling before the application for the landlord's licence or consent is made.

(1C) Subsection (1A) shall not, however, apply to any such agreement to the extent that any circumstances or conditions specified in it are framed by reference to any matter falling to be determined by the landlord or by any other person for the purposes of the agreement, unless under the terms of the agreement—

(a) that person's power to determine that matter is required to be exercised reasonably, or

(b) the tenant is given an unrestricted right to have any such determination reviewed by a person independent of both landlord and tenant whose identity is ascertainable by reference to the agreement,

and in the latter case the agreement provides for the determination made by any such independent person on the review to be conclusive as to the matter in question.

(1D) In its application to a qualifying lease, subsection (1)(b) of this section shall not have effect in relation to any assignment of the lease.

(1E) In subsections (1A) and (1D) of this section—

(a) 'qualifying lease' means any lease which is a new tenancy for the purposes of section 1 of the Landlord and Tenant (Covenants) Act 1995 other than a residential lease, namely a lease by which a building or part of a building is let wholly or mainly as a single private residence; and

(b) references to assignment include parting with possession on assignment.

(2) In all leases whether made before or after the commencement of this Act containing a covenant condition or agreement against the making of improvements without licence or consent, such covenant condition or agreement shall be deemed, notwithstanding any express provision to the contrary, to be subject to a proviso that such licence or consent is not to be unreasonably withheld; but this proviso does not preclude the right to require as a condition of such licence or consent the payment of a reasonable sum in respect of any damage to or diminution in the value of the premises or any neighbouring premises belonging to the landlord, and of any legal or other expenses properly incurred in connection with such licence or consent nor, in the case of an improvement which does not add to the letting value of the holding, does it preclude the right to require as a condition of such licence or consent, where such a requirement would be reasonable, an undertaking on the part of the tenant to reinstate the premises in the condition in which they were before the improvement was executed.

(3) In all leases whether made before or after the commencement of this Act containing a covenant condition or agreement against the alteration of the user of the demised premises, without licence or consent, such covenant condition or agreement shall, if the alteration does not involve any structural alteration of the premises, be deemed, notwithstanding any express provision to the contrary, to be subject to a proviso that no fine or sum of money in

the nature of a fine, whether by way of increase of rent or otherwise, shall be payable for or in respect of such licence or consent; but this proviso does not preclude the right of the landlord to require payment of a reasonable sum in respect of any damage to or diminution in the value of the premises or any neighbouring premises belonging to him and of any legal or other expenses incurred in connection with such licence or consent.

Where a dispute as to the reasonableness of any such sum has been determined by a court of competent jurisdiction, the landlord shall be bound to grant the licence or consent on payment of the sum so determined to be reasonable.

(4) This section shall not apply to leases of agricultural holdings within the meaning of the Agricultural Holdings Act 1986 which are leases in relation to which that Act applies, or to farm business tenancies within the meaning of the Agricultural Tenancies Act 1995, and paragraph (b) of subsection (1), subsection (2) and subsection (3) of this section shall not apply to mining leases.

20. Apportionment of rents

(1) An order of apportionment of a rent reserved by a lease or any such other rent or payment as is mentioned in section ten of the Inclosure Act, 1854, may be made by the Minister of Agriculture and Fisheries under sections ten to fourteen of that Act, on the application of any person interested in the rent or payment, or any part thereof, or in the land in respect of which such rent or payment is payable, without the concurrence of any other person:

Provided that the Minister may in any such case, on the application of any person entitled to the rent or payment or any part thereof, require as a condition of making the order that any apportioned part of the rent or payment which does not exceed the yearly sum of £5 shall be redeemed forthwith in accordance with sections 8 to 10 of the Rentcharges Act 1977 (which, for the purposes of this section, shall have effect with the necessary modifications).

(1A) An order of apportionment under sections 10 to 14 of the said Act of 1854 may provide for the amount apportioned to any part of the land in respect of which the rent or payment is payable to be nil.

(2) Where the reason for the application was due to any action taken by a person other than the applicant, the Minister shall, notwithstanding anything in section fourteen of the Inclosure Act, 1854, have power to direct by whom and in what manner the expenses of the application or any part thereof are to be paid.

23. Service of notices

(1) Any notice, request, demand or other instrument under this Act shall be in writing and may be served on the person on whom it is to be served

either personally, or by leaving it for him at his last known place of abode in England or Wales, or by sending it through the post in a registered letter addressed to him there, or, in the case of a local or public authority or a statutory or a public utility company, to the secretary or other proper officer at the principal office of such authority or company, and in the case of a notice to a landlord, the person on whom it is to be served shall include any agent of the landlord duly authorised in that behalf.

(2) Unless or until a tenant of a holding shall have received notice that the person theretofore entitled to the rents and profits of the holding (hereinafter referred to as 'the original landlord') has ceased to be so entitled, and also notice of the name and address of the person who has become entitled to such rents and profits, any claim, notice, request, demand, or other instrument which the tenant shall serve upon or deliver to the original landlord shall be deemed to have been served upon or delivered to the landlord of such holding.

Appendix 3

Statutory Instruments

Landlord and Tenant (Covenants) Act 1995 (Notices) Regulations 1995

SI 1995/2964

Made	*9th November 1995*
Laid before Parliament	*20th November 1995*
Coming into force	*1st January 1996*

The Lord Chancellor, in exercise of the powers conferred on him by section 27 of the Landlord and Tenant (Covenants) Act 1995, hereby makes the following Regulations:

1.—(1) These Regulations may be cited as the Landlord and Tenant (Covenants) Act 1995 (Notices) Regulations 1995 and shall come into force on 1st January 1996.

(2) In these Regulations, 'the Act' means the Landlord and Tenant (Covenants) Act 1995, and a form referred to by number means the form so numbered in the Schedule to these Regulations.

2. The forms prescribed for the purposes of the Act shall be as follows, or in each case a form substantially to the like effect:

PURPOSE OF NOTICE	FORM TO BE USED
(a) (i) Landlord informing a former tenant or guarantor of such a tenant of an amount payable in respect of a fixed charge under a covenant of the tenancy which the landlord intends to recover from that person under section 17 of the Act	Form 1
(ii) Landlord informing a former tenant or guarantor of such a tenant of a revised, greater amount payable in respect of a	Form 2

PURPOSE OF NOTICE	FORM TO BE USED
fixed charge under a covenant of the tenancy which the landlord intends to recover from that person under section 17 of the Act	
(b) (i) Landlord applying to be released from all the landlord covenants of the tenancy on assignment of his entire interest under sections 6 and 8 of the Act	Whole of Form 3 (landlord to complete Part I only)
(ii) Tenant objecting to the landlord's release under section 8 of the Act	Part II of Form 3
(iii) Tenant consenting to the landlord's release and withdrawing a notice objecting to such release under section 8 of the Act	Notice in writing stating that tenant is now consenting and that the notice of objection is withdrawn
(c) (i) Landlord applying to be released from the landlord covenants of the tenancy to the appropriate extent on assignment of part only of his interest under sections 6 and 8 of the Act	Whole of Form 4 (landlord to complete Part I only)
(ii) Tenant objecting to the landlord's release under section 8 of the Act	Part II of Form 4
(iii) Tenant consenting to the landlord's release and withdrawing a notice objecting to such release under section 8 of the Act	Notice in writing stating that tenant is now consenting and that the notice of objection is withdrawn
(d) (i) Former landlord applying to be released from all the landlord covenants of the tenancy on a subsequent assignment of the landlord's interest under sections 7 and 8 of the Act	Whole of Form 5 (landlord to complete Part I only)
(ii) Tenant objecting to the former landlord's release under section 8 of the Act	Part II of Form 5

PURPOSE OF NOTICE	FORM TO BE USED
(iii) Tenant consenting to the former landlord's release and withdrawing a notice objecting to such release under section 8 of the Act	Notice in writing stating that tenant is now consenting and that the notice of objection is withdrawn
(e) (i) Former landlord who assigned part only of his interest applying to be released from the landlord covenants of the tenancy to the appropriate extent on a subsequent assignment of the landlord's interest under sections 7 and 8 of the Act	Whole of Form 6 (landlord to complete Part I only)
(ii) Tenant objecting to the former landlord's release under section 8 of the Act	Part II of Form 6
(iii) Tenant consenting to the former landlord's release and withdrawing a notice objecting to such release under section 8 of the Act	Notice in writing stating that tenant is now consenting and that the notice of objection is withdrawn
(f) (i) Tenant and tenant's assignee jointly applying for an apportionment of liability under the covenants of the tenancy to become binding on the appropriate person under sections 9 and 10 of the Act	Whole of Form 7 (tenant and assignee to complete Part I only)
(ii) Appropriate person objecting to the apportionment becoming binding on that person under section 10 of the Act	Part II of Form 7
(iii) Appropriate person consenting to the apportionment becoming binding on that person and withdrawing a notice objecting to the apportionment becoming so binding under section 10 of the Act	Notice in writing stating that appropriate person is now consenting and that the notice of objection is withdrawn

PURPOSE OF NOTICE	FORM TO BE USED
(g) (i) Landlord and landlord's assignee jointly applying for an apportionment of liability under the covenants of the tenancy to become binding on the appropriate person under sections 9 and 10 of the Act	Whole of Form 8 (landlord and assignee to complete Part I only)
(ii) Appropriate person objecting to the apportionment becoming binding on that person under section 10 of the Act	Part II of Form 8
(iii) Appropriate person consenting to the apportionment becoming binding on that person and withdrawing a notice objecting to the apportionment becoming so binding under section 10 of the Act	Notice in writing stating that appropriate person is now consenting and that the notice of objection is withdrawn

Dated 9th November 1995   *Mackay of Clashfern, C.*

SCHEDULE

FORM 1

NOTICE TO FORMER TENANT OR GUARANTOR OF INTENTION TO RECOVER FIXED CHARGE[1]
(Landlord and Tenant (Covenants) Act 1995, section 17)

To [name and address]: ....

....

> IMPORTANT — THE PERSON GIVING THIS NOTICE IS PROTECT-
> ING THE RIGHT TO RECOVER THE AMOUNT(S) SPECIFIED
> FROM YOU NOW OR AT SOME TIME IN THE FUTURE. THERE
> MAY BE ACTION WHICH YOU CAN TAKE TO PROTECT YOUR
> POSITION. READ THE NOTICE AND ALL THE NOTES OVERLEAF
> CAREFULLY. IF YOU ARE IN ANY DOUBT ABOUT THE ACTION
> YOU SHOULD TAKE, SEEK ADVICE IMMEDIATELY, FOR IN-
> STANCE FROM A SOLICITOR OR CITIZENS ADVICE BUREAU.

1.   This notice is given under section 17 of the Landlord and Tenant (Covenants) Act 1995. *[see Note 1]*

2.   It relates to (address and description of property) ....

....

let under a lease dated .... and made between ....

....

....

[of which you were formerly tenant] [in relation to which you are liable as guarantor of a person who was formerly tenant].[2]

3.   I/we as landlord[3] hereby give you notice that the fixed charge(s) of which details are set out in the attached Schedule[4] is/are now due and unpaid, and

---

[1] The Act defines a fixed charge as (a) rent, (b) any service charge (as defined by section 18 of the Landlord and Tenant Act 1985, disregarding the words 'of a dwelling') and (c) any amount payable under a tenant covenant of the tenancy providing for payment of a liquidated sum in the event of failure to comply with the covenant.

[2] Delete alternative as appropriate.

[3] 'Landlord' for these purposes includes any person who has the right to enforce the charge.

[4] The Schedule must be in writing, and must indicate in relation to each item the date on which it became payable, the amount payable and whether it is rent, service charge or a fixed charge of some other kind (in which case particulars of the nature of the charge should be given). Charges due before 1 January 1996 are deemed to have become due on that date, but the actual date on which they became due should also be stated.

that I/we intend to recover from you the amount(s) specified in the Schedule [and interest from the date and calculated on the basis specified in the Schedule][5]. *[see Notes 2 and 3]*

4.[6]   There is a possibility that your liability in respect of the fixed charge(s) detailed in the Schedule will subsequently be determined to be for a greater amount. *[see Note 4]*

5.   All correspondence about this notice should be sent to the landlord/landlord's agent at the address given below.

Date .... Signature of landlord/landlord's agent ....
Name and address of landlord ....
....
....
[Name and address of agent ....
....
....]

NOTES

1.   The person giving you this notice alleges that you are still liable for the performance of the tenant's obligations under the tenancy to which this notice relates, either as a previous tenant bound by privity of contract or an authorised guarantee agreement, or because you are the guarantor of a previous tenant. By giving you this notice, the landlord (or other person entitled to enforce payment, such as a management company) is protecting his right to require you to pay the amount specified in the notice. There may be other sums not covered by the notice which the landlord can also recover because they are not fixed charges (for example in respect of repairs or costs if legal proceedings have to be brought). If you pay the amount specified in this notice in full, you will have the right to call on the landlord to grant you an 'overriding lease', which puts you in the position of landlord to the present tenant. There are both advantages and drawbacks to doing this, and you should take advice before coming to a decision.

---

[5] Delete words in brackets if not applicable. If applicable, the Schedule must state the basis on which interest is calculated (for example, rate of interest, date from which it is payable and provision of Lease or other document under which it is payable).
[6] Delete this paragraph if not applicable. If applicable (for example, where there is an outstanding rent review or service charge collected on account) a further notice must be served on the former tenant or guarantor within three (3) months beginning with the date on which the greater amount is determined. If only applicable to one or more charge of several, the Schedule should specify which.

Validity of notice

2.   The landlord is required to give this notice within six months of the date on which the charge or charges in question became due (or, if it became due before 1 January 1996, within six months of that date). If the notice has been given late, it is not valid and the amount in the notice cannot be recovered from you. The date of the giving of the notice may not be the date written on the notice or the date on which you actually saw it. It may, for instance, be the date on which the notice was delivered through the post to your last address known to the landlord. If you are in any doubt, you should seek advice immediately.

Interest

3.   If interest is payable on the amount due, the landlord does not have to state the precise amount of interest, but he must state the basis on which the interest is calculated to enable you to work out the likely amount, or he will not be able to claim interest at all. This does not include interest which may be payable under rules of court if legal proceedings are brought.

Change in amount due

4.   Apart from interest, the landlord is not entitled to recover an amount which is more than he has specified in the notice, with one exception. This is where the amount cannot be finally determined within six months after it is due (for example, if there is dispute concerning an outstanding rent review or if the charge is a service charge collected on account and adjusted following final determination). In such a case, if the amount due is eventually determined to be more than originally notified, the landlord may claim the larger amount *if and only if* he completes the paragraph giving notice of the possibility that the amount may change, and gives a further notice specifying the larger amount within three months of the final determination.

FORM 2

FURTHER NOTICE TO FORMER TENANT OR GUARANTOR OF REVISED AMOUNT DUE IN RESPECT OF A FIXED CHARGE[1]
(Landlord and Tenant (Covenants) Act 1995, section 17)

To [name and address]: ....
....

> IMPORTANT — THE PERSON GIVING THIS NOTICE IS PRO-
> TECTING THE RIGHT TO RECOVER THE AMOUNT(S) SPECI-
> FIED FROM YOU NOW OR AT SOME TIME IN THE FUTURE.
> THERE MAY BE ACTION WHICH YOU CAN TAKE TO PROTECT
> YOUR POSITION. READ THE NOTICE AND ALL THE NOTES
> OVERLEAF CAREFULLY. IF YOU ARE IN ANY DOUBT ABOUT
> THE ACTION YOU SHOULD TAKE, SEEK ADVICE IMMEDIATE-
> LY, FOR INSTANCE FROM A SOLICITOR OR CITIZENS ADVICE
> BUREAU.

1.   This notice is given under section 17 of the Landlord and Tenant
(Covenants) Act 1995. *[see Note 1]*

2.   It relates to (address and description of property) ....
....
let under a lease dated .... and made between ....
....
....
[of which you were formerly tenant] [in relation to which you are liable as
guarantor of a person who was formerly tenant].[2]

3.   You were informed on .... (date of original notice)
of the amount due in respect of a fixed charge or charges, and of the
possibility that your liability in respect of the charge(s) might subsequently
be determined to be for a greater amount.

---

[1] The Act defines a fixed charge as (a) rent, (b) any service charge (as defined by section 18 of
the Landlord and Tenant Act 1985, disregarding the words 'of a dwelling') and (c) any amount
payable under a tenant covenant of the tenancy providing for payment of a liquidated sum in
the event of failure to comply with the covenant.
[2] Delete alternative as appropriate.

4. I/we as landlord[3] hereby give you notice that the fixed charge(s) of which details are set out in the attached Schedule[4] has/have now been determined to be for a greater amount than specified in the original notice, and that I/we intend to recover from you the amount(s) specified in the Schedule [and interest from the date and calculated on the basis specified in the Schedule].[5] *[see Notes 2 and 3]*

5. All correspondence about this notice should be sent to the landlord/ landlord's agent at the address given below.

Date .... Signature of landlord/landlord's agent ....
Name and address of landlord ....
....
....
[Name and address of agent ....
....
....]

NOTES

1. The person giving you this notice alleges that you are still liable for the performance of the tenant's obligations under the tenancy to which this notice relates, either as a previous tenant bound by privity of contract or an authorised guarantee agreement, or because you are the guarantor of a previous tenant. You should already have been given a notice by which the landlord (or other person entitled to enforce payment, such as a management company) protected his right to require you to pay the amount specified in that notice. The purpose of this notice is to protect the landlord's right to require you to pay a larger amount, because the amount specified in the original notice could not be finally determined at the time of the original notice (for example, because there was a dispute concerning an outstanding rent review or if the charge was a service charge collected on account and adjusted following final determination).

Validity of notice
2. The notice is not valid unless the original notice contained a warning that the amount in question might subsequently be determined to be greater.

---

[3] 'Landlord' for these purposes includes any person who has the right to enforce the charge.
[4] The Schedule can be in any form, but must indicate in relation to each item the date on which it was revised, the revised amount payable and whether it is rent, service charge or a fixed charge of some other kind (in which case particulars of the nature of the charge should be given).
[5] Delete words in brackets if not applicable. If applicable, the Schedule must state the basis on which interest is calculated (for example, rate of interest, date from which it is payable and provision of Lease or other document under which it is payable).

In addition, the landlord is required to give this notice within three months of the date on which the amount was finally determined. If the original notice did not include that warning, or if this notice has been given late, then this notice is not valid and the landlord cannot recover the greater amount, but only the smaller amount specified in the original notice. The date of the giving of this notice may not be the date written on the notice or the date on which you actually saw it. It may, for instance, be the date on which the notice was delivered through the post to your last address known to the person giving notice. If you are in any doubt, you should seek advice immediately.

Interest
3.   If interest is chargeable on the amount due, the landlord does not have to state the precise amount of interest, but he must have stated the basis on which the interest is calculated, or he will not be able to claim interest at all.

FORM 3

PART I

LANDLORD'S NOTICE APPLYING FOR RELEASE FROM LANDLORD COVENANTS OF A TENANCY ON ASSIGNMENT OF WHOLE OF REVERSION
(Landlord and Tenant (Covenants) Act 1995, sections 6 and 8)

To [name and address]: ....

....

IMPORTANT — THIS NOTICE IS INTENDED TO RELEASE YOUR LANDLORD FROM HIS OBLIGATIONS WHEN HE TRANSFERS HIS INTEREST TO A NEW LANDLORD. IF YOU CONSIDER THAT THERE IS GOOD REASON FOR YOUR LAND-LORD **NOT** TO BE RELEASED, YOU MUST ACT QUICKLY. READ THE NOTICE AND ALL THE NOTES OVERLEAF CARE-FULLY. IF YOU ARE IN ANY DOUBT ABOUT THE ACTION YOU SHOULD TAKE, SEEK ADVICE IMMEDIATELY, FOR INSTANCE FROM A SOLICITOR OR CITIZENS ADVICE BUREAU.

1. This notice is given under section 8 of the Landlord and Tenant (Covenants) Act 1995. *[see Note 1]*

2. It relates to (address and description of property) ....

....

let under a lease dated .... and made between ....

....

of which you are the tenant.

3. I/we [propose to transfer] [transferred on ....]¹ the whole of the landlord's interest and wish to be released from the landlord's obligations under the tenancy with effect from the date of the transfer. *[see Note 2]*

4. If you consider that it is reasonable for me/us to be released, you do not need to do anything, but it would help me/us if you notify me/us using Part I of this Form. *[see Note 3]*

5. If you do **not** consider it reasonable for me/us to be released, you **must** notify me/us of your objection, using Part II of this Form, within the period of **FOUR WEEKS** beginning with the giving of this notice, or I/we will be

---

¹ Delete alternative as appropriate.

released in any event. You may withdraw your objection at any time by notifying me/us in writing. *[see Notes 4–6]*

6. All correspondence about this notice should be sent to the landlord/landlord's agent at the address given below.

Date .... Signature of landlord/landlord's agent ....
Name and address of landlord ....
....
....
[Name and address of agent ....
....
....]

NOTES TO PART I

Release of landlord
1. The landlord is about to transfer his interest to a new landlord, or has just done so, and is applying to be released from the obligations of the landlord under your tenancy. You have a number of options: you may expressly agree to the landlord's being released; you may object to his being released (with the option of withdrawing your objection later); or you may do nothing, in which case the landlord will automatically be released, with effect from the date of the transfer, once four weeks have elapsed from the date of the giving of the notice. If you choose to oppose release, you must act within four weeks of the giving of the notice.

Validity of notice
2. The landlord must give this notice either before the transfer or within the period of four weeks beginning with the date of the transfer. If the notice has been given late, it is not valid. You should read Note 4 below concerning the date of the giving of the notice.

Agreeing to release
3. If you are content for the landlord to be released, you may notify him of this using Part II of this Form, and the landlord will then be released as from the date of the transfer. If you do this, you may not later change your mind and object.

Objecting to release
4. If you think that it is not reasonable for the landlord to be released, you may object to release by notifying the landlord, using Part II of this Form. You must, however, do this within four weeks of the date of the giving of

the notice. The date of the giving of the notice may not be the date written on the notice or the date on which you actually saw it. It may, for instance, be the date on which the notice was delivered through the post to your last address known by the landlord. If there has been any delay in your seeing this notice you may need to act very quickly. If you are in any doubt, you should seek advice immediately. If you change your mind after objecting, you may consent instead, at any time, by notifying the landlord *in writing* that you now consent to his being released and that your objection is withdrawn.

5. If you object within the time limit, the landlord will only be released if *either* he applies to a court and the court decides that it is reasonable for him to be released, *or* you withdraw your objection by a notice in writing as explained in Note 4 above.

6. In deciding whether to object, you should bear in mind that if the court finds that it is reasonable for the landlord to be released, or if you withdraw your objection late, you may have to pay costs.

PART II

TENANT'S RESPONSE TO LANDLORD'S NOTICE APPLYING FOR RELEASE FROM LANDLORD COVENANTS OF A TENANCY ON ASSIGNMENT OF WHOLE OF REVERSION
(Landlord and Tenant (Covenants) Act 1995, section 8)

To [name and address]: ....

....

1. This notice is given under section 8 of the Landlord and Tenant (Covenants) Act 1995.

2. It relates to (address and description of property) ....

....

let under a lease dated .... and made between ....

....

....

Of which you are the landlord or have just transferred the landlord's interest.

3. You [propose to transfer] [transferred on ....]¹ the landlord's interest and have applied to be released from the landlord's obligations under the tenancy with effect from the date of the transfer.

4.² I/we agree to your being released from the landlord's obligations with effect from the date of the transfer. *[see Note 1]*

OR

4. I/we do **not** consider it reasonable that you should be released from the landlord's obligations, and object to the release. *[see Notes 2 and 3]*

5. All correspondence about this notice should be sent to the tenant/tenant's agent at the address given below.

Date .... Signature of tenant/tenant's agent ....
Name and address of tenant ....

....

....

[Name and address of agent ....

....

....]

---

¹ Delete alternative as appropriate.
² The tenant should select one version of paragraph 4 and cross out the other.

NOTES TO PART II

Agreement to release

1. If the tenant has indicated agreement in paragraph 4 of the notice, you will automatically be released from the landlord's obligations under the tenancy with effect from the date of your transfer of the landlord's interest.

Objection to release

2. If the tenant has indicated an objection in paragraph 4 of the notice, you will not be released unless either the tenant later withdraws his objection *or* you apply to the Country Court to declare that it is reasonable for you to be released, and the court so declares. If you are not released, you may still apply for release when the landlord's interest, or part of it, is next transferred, and it may therefore be sensible to make arrangements for the person to whom you are making the transfer to inform you when he intends to transfer the landlord's interest in his turn.

Validity of notice of objection

3. A notice of objection by the tenant is only valid if he has given it to you within the period of four weeks beginning with the date on which you gave him your notice applying for release. If you are in any doubt, you should seek advice before applying to the court.

FORM 4

PART I

LANDLORD'S NOTICE APPLYING FOR RELEASE FROM LANDLORD COVENANTS OF A TENANCY ON ASSIGNMENT OF PART OF REVERSION
(Landlord and Tenant (Covenants) Act 1995, sections 6 and 8)

To [name and address]: ....

....

IMPORTANT — THIS NOTICE IS INTENDED TO RELEASE YOUR LANDLORD PARTLY FROM HIS OBLIGATIONS WHEN HE TRANSFERS PART OF HIS INTEREST TO A NEW LANDLORD. IF YOU CONSIDER THAT THERE IS GOOD REASON FOR YOUR LANDLORD **NOT** TO BE RELEASED, YOU MUST ACT QUICKLY. READ THE NOTICE AND ALL THE NOTES OVER LEAF CARE-FULLY. IF YOU ARE IN ANY DOUBT ABOUT THE ACTION YOU SHOULD TAKE, SEEK ADVICE IMMEDIATELY, FOR INSTANCE FROM A SOLICITOR OR CITIZENS ADVICE BUREAU.

---

1. This notice is given under section 8 of the Landlord and Tenant (Covenants) Act 1995. *[see Note 1]*

2. It relates to (address and description of property) ....

....

let under a lease dated .... and made between ....

....

....

of which you are the tenant.

3. I/we [propose to transfer] [transferred on ....]¹
part of the landlord's interest, namely ....
and wish to be released from the landlord's obligations under the tenancy, to the extent that they fall to be complied with in relation to that part, with effect from the date of the transfer. *[see Note 2]*

4. If you consider that it is reasonable for me/us to be released, you do not need to do anything, but it would help me/us if you notify me/us using Part II of this Form. *[see Note 3]*

---

¹ Delete alternative as appropriate.

5. If you do **not** consider it reasonable for me/us to be released, you **must** notify me/us of your objection, using Part II of this Form, within the period of **FOUR WEEKS** beginning with the giving of this notice, or I/we will be released in any event. You may withdraw your objection at any time by notifying me/us in writing. *[see Notes 4–6]*

6. All correspondence about this notice should be sent to the landlord/ landlord's agent at the address given below.

Date .... Signature of landlord/landlord's agent ....
Name and address of landlord ....
....
....
[Name and address of agent ....
....
....]

NOTES TO PART I

Release of landlord
1. The landlord is about to transfer part of his interest to a new landlord, or has just done so, and is applying to be released from the obligations of the landlord under your tenancy, to the extent that they fall to be complied with in relation to that part. You have a number of options: you may expressly agree to the landlord's being released; you may object to his being released (with the option of withdrawing your objection later); or you may do nothing, in which case the landlord will automatically be released, with effect from the date of the assignment, once four weeks have elapsed from the date of the giving of the notice. If you choose to oppose release, you must act within four weeks of the giving of the notice.

Validity of notice
2. The landlord must give this notice either before the transfer or within the period of four weeks beginning with the date of the transfer. If the notice has been given late, it is not valid. You should read Note 4 below concerning the date of the giving of the notice.

Agreeing to release
3. If you are content for the landlord to be released, you may notify him of this using Part II of this Form, and the landlord will then be released as from the date of the transfer. If you do this, you may not later change your mind and object.

Objecting to release

4.   If you think that it is not reasonable for the landlord to be released, you may object to release by notifying the landlord, using Part II of this Form. You must, however, do this within four weeks of the date of the giving of the notice. The date of the giving of the notice may not be the date written on the notice or the date on which you actually saw it. It may, for instance, be the date on which the notice was delivered through the post to your last address known to the person giving the notice. If there has been any delay in your seeing this notice you may need to act very quickly. If you are in any doubt, you should seek advice immediately. If you change your mind after objecting, you may consent instead, at any time, by notifying the landlord *in writing* that you now consent to his being released and that your objection is withdrawn.

5.   If you object within the time limit, the landlord will only be released if *either* he applies to a court and the court decides that it is reasonable for him to be released, *or* you withdraw your objection by a notice in writing as explained in Note 4 above.

6.   In deciding whether to object, you should bear in mind that if the court finds that it is reasonable for the landlord to be released, or if you withdraw your objection late, you may have to pay costs.

PART II

TENANT'S RESPONSE TO LANDLORD'S NOTICE APPLYING FOR RELEASE FROM LANDLORD COVENANTS OF A TENANCY ON ASSIGNMENT OF PART OF REVERSION
(Landlord and Tenant (Covenants) Act 1995, section 8)

To [name and address]: ....
....

1.   This notice is given under section 8 of the Landlord and Tenant (Covenants) Act 1995.

2.   It relates to (address and description of property) ....
....
let under a lease dated .... and made between ....
....
....
of which you are the landlord or have just transferred part of the landlord's interest.

3.   You [propose to transfer] [transferred on ....]¹
part of the landlord's interest, namely ....
and have applied to be released from the landlord's obligations under the tenancy, to the extent that they fall to be complied with in relation to that part, with effect from the date of the transfer.

4.²   I/we agree to your being released from the landlord's obligations to that extent with effect from the date of the transfer. *[see Note 1]*

OR

4.   I/we do **not** consider it reasonable that you should be released from the landlord's obligations, and object to the release. *[see Notes 2 and 3]*

5.   All correspondence about this notice should be sent to the tenant/tenant's agent at the address given below.

Date .... Signature of tenant/tenant's agent ....
Name and address of tenant ....
....
....

---

¹ Delete alternative as appropriate.
² The tenant should select one version of paragraph 4 and cross out the other.

[Name and address of agent ....
....
....]

NOTES TO PART II

Agreement to release
1.   If the tenant has indicated agreement in paragraph 4 of the notice, you
will automatically be released from the landlord's obligations under the
tenancy, to the extent that they fall to be complied with in relation to the part
of your interest being transferred, with effect from the date of the transfer.

Objection to release
2.   If the tenant has indicated an objection in paragraph 4 of the notice, you
will not be released unless *either* the tenant later withdraws his objection *or*
you apply to the County Court to declare that it is reasonable for you to be
released, and the court so declares. If you are not released, you may still
apply for release when the landlord's interest, or part of it, is next transferred,
and it may therefore be sensible to make arrangements for the person to
whom you are making the transfer to inform you when he intends to transfer
the landlord's interest in his turn.

Validity of notice of objection
3.   A notice of objection by the tenant is only valid if he has given it to you
within the period of four weeks beginning with the date on which you gave
him your notice applying for release. If you are in any doubt, you should
seek advice before applying to the court.

FORM 5

PART I

FORMER LANDLORD'S NOTICE APPLYING FOR RELEASE FROM LANDLORD COVENANTS OF A TENANCY
(Landlord and Tenant (Covenants) Act 1995, sections 7 and 8)

To [name and address]: ....
....

> IMPORTANT — THIS NOTICE IS INTENDED TO RELEASE THE FORMER LANDLORD OF THE PROPERTY FROM HIS OBLIGATIONS UNDER YOUR TENANCY. IF YOU CONSIDER THAT THERE IS GOOD REASON FOR THE FORMER LANDLORD **NOT** TO BE RELEASED, YOU MUST ACT QUICKLY. READ THE NOTICE AND ALL THE NOTES OVERLEAF CAREFULLY. IF YOU ARE IN ANY DOUBT ABOUT THE ACTION YOU SHOULD TAKE, SEEK ADVICE IMMEDIATELY, FOR INSTANCE FROM A SOLICITOR OR CITIZENS ADVICE BUREAU.

1. This notice is given under section 8 of the Landlord and Tenant (Covenants) Act 1995. *[see Note 1]*

2. It relates to (address and description of property) ....
....
let under a lease dated .... and made between ....
....
....
of which you are the tenant.

3. I/we was/were formerly landlord of the property of which you are tenant and remained bound by the landlord's obligations under the tenancy after transferring the landlord's interest. The landlord's interest, or part of it [is about to be transferred] [was transferred on][1]. I/we wish to be released from my/our obligations with effect from the date of that transfer. *[see Note 2]*

4. If you consider that it is reasonable for me/us to be released, you do not need to do anything, but it would help me/us if you notify me/us using Part II of this Form. *[see Note 3]*

5. If you do **not** consider it reasonable for me/us to be released, you **must** notify me/us of your objection, using Part II of this Form, within the period

---

[1] Delete alternative as appropriate.

of **FOUR WEEKS** beginning with the giving of this notice, or I/we will be released in any event. You may withdraw your objection at any time by notifying me/us in writing. *[see Notes 4—6]*

6.   All correspondence about this notice should be sent to the former landlord/former landlord's agent at the address given below.

Date .... Signature of former landlord/agent ....
Name and address of former landlord ....
....
....
[Name and address of agent ....
....
....]

NOTES TO PART I

Release of former landlord
1.   Your landlord is about to transfer his interest, or part of it, to a new landlord, or has just done so, and a former landlord of the property is applying to be released from his obligations, from which he was not released when he transferred the landlord's interest himself. You have a number of options: you may expressly agree to the former landlord's being released; you may object to his being released (with the option of withdrawing your objection later); or you may do nothing, in which case the former landlord will automatically be released, with effect from the date of the present transfer, once four weeks have elapsed from the date of the giving of the notice. If you choose to oppose release, you must act within four weeks of the giving of the notice.

Validity of notice
2.   The former landlord is required to give this notice either before the transfer by the present landlord takes place or within the period of four weeks beginning with the date of the transfer. If the notice has been given late, it is not valid. You should read Note 4 below concerning the date of the giving of the notice.

Agreeing to release
3.   If you are content for the former landlord to be released, you may notify him of this using Part II of this Form, and the former landlord will then automatically be released as from the date of the present transfer. If you do this, you may not later change your mind and object.

Objecting to release

4.   If you think that it is not reasonable for the former landlord to be released, you may object to release by notifying the former landlord, using Part II of this Form. You must, however, do this within four weeks of the date of the giving of the notice. The date of the giving of the notice may not be the date written on the notice or the date on which you actually saw it. It may, for instance, be the date on which the notice was delivered through the post to your last address known to the person giving the notice. If there has been any delay in your seeing this notice you may need to act very quickly. If you are in any doubt, you should seek advice immediately. If you change your mind after objecting, you may consent instead, at any time, by notifying the former landlord *in writing* that you now consent to his being released and that your objection is withdrawn.

5.   If you object within the time limit, the former landlord will only be released if *either* he applies to a court and the court decides that it is reasonable for him to be released, *or* you withdraw your objection by a notice in writing as explained in Note 4 above.

6.   In deciding whether to object, you should bear in mind that if the court finds that it is reasonable for the former landlord to be released, or if you withdraw your objection late, you may have to pay costs.

PART II

TENANT'S RESPONSE TO FORMER LANDLORD'S NOTICE APPLYING FOR RELEASE FROM LANDLORD COVENANTS OF A TENANCY
(Landlord and Tenant (Covenants) Act 1995, section 8)

To [name and address]: ....

....

1. This notice is given under section 8 of the Landlord and Tenant (Covenants) Act 1995.

2. It relates to (address and description of property) ....

....

let under a lease dated .... and made between ....

....

....

of which you were formerly landlord.

3. You have applied to be released from the landlord's obligations under the tenancy with effect from the date of a [proposed transfer] [transfer on ....][1] of the landlord's interest.

4.[2] I/we agree to your being released from the landlord's obligations with effect from the date of that transfer. *[see Note 1]*

OR

4. I/we do **not** consider it reasonable that you should be released from the landlord's obligations, and object to your being so released. *[see Notes 2 and 3]*

5. All correspondence about this notice should be sent to the tenant/tenant's agent at the address given below.

Date .... Signature of tenant/tenant's agent ....
Name and address of tenant ....
....
....
[Name and address of agent ....
....
....]

---

[1] Delete alternative as appropriate.
[2]. The tenant should select one version of paragraph 4 and cross out the other.

NOTES TO PART II

Agreement to release
1.   If the tenant has indicated agreement in paragraph 4 of the notice, you will automatically be released from the landlord's obligations under the tenancy with effect from the date of the transfer by the present landlord.

Objection to release
2.   If the tenant has indicated an objection in paragraph 4 of the notice, you will not be released unless *either* the tenant later withdraws his objection *or* you apply to the County Court to declare that it is reasonable for you to be released, and the court so declares. If you are not released, you may still apply for release when the reversion, or part of it, is next assigned, and it may therefore be sensible to make arrangements for you to be informed when the present landlord's transferee intends to transfer the landlord's interest in his turn.

Validity of notice of objection
3.   A notice of objection by the tenant is only valid if he has given it to you within the period of four weeks beginning with the date on which you gave him your notice applying for release. If you are in any doubt, you should seek advice before applying to the court.

FORM 6

PART I

FORMER LANDLORD'S NOTICE APPLYING FOR RELEASE FROM LANDLORD COVENANTS OF A TENANCY (FORMER LANDLORD HAVING ASSIGNED PART OF REVERSION)
(Landlord and Tenant (Covenants) Act 1995, sections 7 and 8)

To [name and address]: ....
....

> IMPORTANT — THIS NOTICE IS INTENDED TO RELEASE THE FORMER LANDLORD OF THE PROPERTY PARTIALLY FROM HIS OBLIGATIONS UNDER YOUR TENANCY. IF YOU CONSIDER THAT THERE IS GOOD REASON FOR THE FORMER LANDLORD **NOT** TO BE RELEASED, YOU MUST ACT QUICKLY. READ THE NOTICE AND ALL THE NOTES OVERLEAF CAREFULLY. IF YOU ARE IN ANY DOUBT ABOUT THE ACTION YOU SHOULD TAKE, SEEK ADVICE IMMEDIATELY, FOR INSTANCE FROM A SOLICITOR OR CITIZENS ADVICE BUREAU.

1. This notice is given under section 8 of the Landlord and Tenant (Covenants) Act 1995. *[see Note 1]*

2. It relates to (address and description of property) ....
....
let under a lease dated .... and made between ....
....
....
of which you are the tenant.

3. I/we was/were formerly landlord of the property of which you are tenant and remained bound by all the landlord's obligations under the tenancy after transferring part of the landlord's interest, namely ....
....
The landlord's interest, or part of it [is about to be transferred] [was transferred on ....]¹
I/we wish to be released from my/our obligations with effect from the date of that transfer. *[see Note 2]*

---

¹ Delete alternative as appropriate.

4. If you consider that it is reasonable for me/us to be released, you do not need to do anything, but it would help me/us if you notify me/us using Part II of this Form. *[see Note 3]*

5. If you do **not** consider it reasonable for me/us to be released, you **must** notify me/us of your objection, using Part II of this Form, within the period of **FOUR WEEKS** beginning with the giving of this notice, or I/we will be released in any event. You may withdraw your objection at any time by notifying me/us in writing. *[see Notes 4–6]*

6. All correspondence about this notice should be sent to the former landlord/former landlord's agent at the address given below.

Date .... Signature of former landlord/agent ....
Name and address of former landlord ....
....
....
[Name and address of agent ....
....
....]

NOTES TO PART I

Release of former landlord
1. Your landlord is about to transfer his interest, or part of it, to a new landlord, or has just done so, and a former landlord of the property is applying to be released from his obligations in relation to part of the landlord' s interest, from which he was not released when he transferred that part himself. You have a number of options: you may expressly agree to the former landlord's being released; you may object to his being released (with the option of withdrawing your objection later); or you may do nothing, in which case the former landlord will automatically be released, with effect from the date of the present transfer, once four weeks have elapsed from the date of the giving of the notice. If you choose to oppose release, you must act within four weeks of the giving of the notice.

Validity of notice
2. The former landlord is required to give this notice either before the transfer by the present landlord takes place or within the period of four weeks beginning with the date of the transfer. If the notice has been given late, it is not valid. You should read Note 4 below concerning the date of the giving of the notice.

Agreeing to release

3.   If you are content for the former landlord to be released, you may notify him of this using Part II of this Form, and the former landlord will then automatically be released as from the date of the present transfer. If you do this, you may not later change your mind and object.

Objecting to release

4.   If you think that it is not reasonable for the former landlord to be released, you may object to release by notifying the former landlord, using Part II of this Form. You must, however, do this within four weeks of the date of the giving of the notice. The date of the giving of the notice may not be the date written on the notice or the date on which you actually saw it. It may, for instance, be the date on which the notice was delivered through the post to your last address known to the person giving the notice. If there has been any delay in your seeing this notice you may need to act very quickly. If you are in any doubt, you should seek advice immediately. If you change your mind after objecting, you may consent instead, at any time, by notifying the former landlord *in writing* that you now consent to his being released and that your objection is withdrawn.

5.   If you object within the time limit, the former landlord will only be released if *either* he applies to a court and the court decides that it is reasonable for him to be released, *or* you withdraw your objection by a notice in writing as explained in Note 4 above.

6.   In deciding whether to object, you should bear in mind that if the court finds that it is reasonable for the former landlord to be released, or if you withdraw your objection late, you may have to pay costs.

PART II

TENANT'S RESPONSE TO FORMER LANDLORD'S NOTICE APPLYING FOR RELEASE FROM LANDLORD COVENANTS OF A TENANCY (FORMER LANDLORD HAVING ASSIGNED PART OF REVERSION)
(Landlord and Tenant (Covenants) Act 1995, section 8)

To [name and address]: ....
....

1. This notice is given under section 8 of the Landlord and Tenant (Covenants) Act 1995.

2. It relates to (address and description of property) ....
....
let under a lease dated .... and made between ....
....
....
of which you were formerly landlord.

3. You remain bound by the landlord's obligations under the tenancy in relation to a part of the landlord's interest which you previously assigned, namely ....
....
You have applied to be released from those obligations, to the extent that they relate to that part, with effect from the date of a [proposed transfer] [transfer on ....]¹ of the landlord's interest.

4.² I/we agree to your being released from the landlord's obligations to that effect from the date of that transfer. *[see Note 1]*

OR

4. I/we do **not** consider it reasonable that you should be released from the landlord's obligations, and object to your being so released. *[see Notes 2 and 3]*

5. All correspondence about this notice should be sent to the tenant/tenant's agent at the address given below.

Date .... Signature of tenant/tenant's agent ....

---

¹ Delete alternative as appropriate.
² The tenant should select one version of paragraph 4 and cross out the other.

Name and address of tenant ....

....

....

[Name and address of agent ....

....

....]

NOTES TO PART II

Agreement to release

1.   If the tenant has indicated agreement in paragraph 4 of the notice, you will automatically be released from the landlord's obligations under the tenancy to the appropriate extent with effect from the date of the transfer by the present landlord.

Objection to release

2.   If the tenant has indicated an objection in paragraph 4 of the notice, you will not be released unless *either* the tenant later withdraws his objection *or* you apply to the County Court to declare that it is reasonable for you to be released, and the court so declares. If you are not released, you may still apply for release when the reversion, or part of it, is next transferred, and it may therefore be sensible to make arrangements for you to be informed when the present landlord's transferee intends to transfer the landlord's interest in his turn.

Validity of notice of objection

3.   A notice of objection by the tenant is only valid if he has given it to you within the period of four weeks beginning with the date on which you gave him your notice applying for release. If you are in any doubt, you should seek advice before applying to the court.

FORM 7

PART I

JOINT NOTICE BY TENANT AND ASSIGNEE FOR BINDING APPORTIONMENT OF LIABILITY UNDER NON-ATTRIBUTABLE TENANT COVENANTS OF A TENANCY ON ASSIGNMENT OF PART OF PROPERTY
(Landlord and Tenant (Covenants) Act 1995, sections 9 and 10)

To [name and address]: ....

....

IMPORTANT — THIS NOTICE IS INTENDED TO AFFECT THE WAY IN WHICH YOU CAN ENFORCE THE TENANT'S OBLIGATIONS UNDER THE TENANCY AS BETWEEN THE TENANT AND THE NEW TENANT. IF YOU CONSIDER THAT THERE IS GOOD REASON WHY YOU SHOULD **NOT** BE BOUND BY THEIR AGREEMENT, YOU MUST ACT QUICKLY. READ THE NOTICE AND ALL THE NOTES OVERLEAF CAREFULLY. IF YOU ARE IN ANY DOUBT ABOUT THE ACTION YOU SHOULD TAKE, SEEK ADVICE IMMEDIATELY, FOR INSTANCE FROM A SOLICITOR OR CITIZENS ADVICE BUREAU.

---

1.   This notice is given under section 10 of the Landlord and Tenant (Covenants) Act 1995. *[see Note 1]*

2.   It relates to (address and description of property) ....

....

let under a lease dated .... and made between ....

....

....

of which you are the landlord.[1]

3.   We are the parties to a [proposed transfer] [transfer on ....][2] of part of the property comprised in the tenancy, namely ....

....

We are jointly and severally liable to perform the obligation(s) specified in the attached Schedule and have agreed to divide that liability between us in

---

[1] 'Landlord', for these purposes, includes any person for the time being entitled to enforce the obligations in question (for example, a management company).
[2] Delete alternative as appropriate.

the manner specified in the Schedule.[3] We wish this agreement to be binding on you as well as between us, with effect from the date of the transfer. *[see Note 2]*

4.   If you consider that it is reasonable for you to be bound by this agreement, you do not need to do anything, but it would help us if you notify us using Part II of this Form. *[see Note 3]*

5.   If you do **not** consider it reasonable for you to be bound by this agreement, you **must** notify both of us of your objection, using Part II of this Form, within the period of **FOUR WEEKS** beginning with the giving of this notice. You may withdraw your objection at any time by notifying us in writing. *[see Notes 4—6]*

6.   All correspondence about this notice should be copied, one copy sent to each of the parties to the agreement, at the addresses given below.

Signature of tenant/tenant's agents ....
Name and address of tenant ....
....
....
[Name and address of agent ....
....
....]
Signature of new tenant/agent ....
Name and address of new tenant ....
....
....
[Name and address of agent ....
....
....]
Date ....

NOTES TO PART I

Apportionment of liability
1.   The tenant is about to transfer, or has just transferred, part of his interest to a new tenant, but they are jointly and severally liable for a particular

---

[3] The Schedule must be in writing, and must specify the nature of the obligation, the term or condition of the Lease or other instrument under which it arises and the manner in which liability to perform it is divided under the agreement (for example, an obligation to pay service charge under a specific provision of the lease might be divided equally). It may be helpful to attach a copy of the agreement to the notice.

obligation or obligations covering the whole of the property. They have agreed to divide that liability between them, and are applying for you as the landlord to be bound as well, so that you can only enforce the liability against each of them as set out in their agreement. If you are bound, any subsequent landlord to whom you may transfer your interest will also be bound. You have a number of options: you may expressly agree to be bound; you may object to being bound (with the option of withdrawing your objection later); or you may do nothing, in which case you will automatically be bound, with effect from the date of the transfer, once four weeks have elapsed from the date of the giving of the notice. If you choose to object, you must act within four weeks of the giving of the notice.

Validity of notice
2.   This notice must be given either before the transfer or within the period of four weeks beginning with the date of the transfer. If the notice has been given late, it is not valid. You should read Note 4 below concerning the date of the giving of the notice.

Agreeing to be bound
3.   If you are content to be bound, you may notify the tenant and new tenant using Part II of this Form (sending a copy to each of them), and all of you will be bound with effect from the date of the transfer. If you do this, you may not later change your mind and object.

Objecting to being bound
4.   If you think that it is not reasonable for you to be bound, you may object by notifying the tenant and new tenant, using Part II of this Form (sending a copy to each of them). You must, however, do this within four weeks of the date of the giving of this notice. The date of the giving of the notice may not be the date written on the notice or the date on which you actually saw it. It may, for instance, be the date on which the notice was delivered through the post to your last address known to the person giving the notice. If there has been any delay in your seeing this notice you may need to act very quickly. If you are in any doubt, you should seek advice immediately. If you change your mind after objecting, you may consent instead, at any time, by notifying *both* the tenant and new tenant *in writing* that you now consent to be bound and that your objection is withdrawn.

5.   If you object within the time limit, the apportionment will only bind you if *either* the tenant and new tenant apply to a court and the court decides that it is reasonable for you to be bound, *or* you withdraw your objection by notice in writing as explained in Note 4 above.

6.   In deciding whether to object, you should bear in mind that if the court finds that it is reasonable for you to be bound, *or* if you withdraw your objection late, you may have to pay costs.

PART II

LANDLORD'S RESPONSE TO JOINT NOTICE BY TENANT AND ASSIGNEE SEEKING BINDING APPORTIONMENT OF LIABILITY UNDER NON-ATTRIBUTABLE TENANT COVENANTS OF A TENANCY ON ASSIGNMENT OF PART OF PROPERTY
(Landlord and Tenant (Covenants) Act 1995, section 10)

To [name and address]: ....

....

And [name and address]: ....

....

1. This notice is given under section 10 of the Landlord and Tenant (Covenants) Act 1995.

2. It relates to (address and description of property) ....

....

let under a lease dated .... and made between ....

....

....

of which I/we am/are the landlord.[1]

3. You have applied for me/us to be bound by your agreement to divide liability between you with effect from the [proposed transfer] [transfer on ....][2] of part of the property comprised in the tenancy.

4.[3] I/we agree to be bound by your agreement with effect from the date of the transfer. *[see Note 1]*

OR

4. I/we do **not** consider it reasonable that I/we should be bound by your agreement, and object to being so bound. *[see Notes 2 and 3]*

6. All correspondence about this notice should be sent to the landlord/ landlord's agent at the address given below.

Date .... Signature of landlord/landlord's agent ....

---

[1] 'Landlord', for these purposes, includes any person for the time being entitled to enforce the obligations in question (for example, a management company).

[2] Delete alternative as appropriate.

[3] The landlord should select one version of paragraph 4 and cross out the other.

Name and address of landlord ....

....

....

[Name and address of agent ....

....

....]

NOTES TO PART II

Agreement to be bound
1.   If the landlord has indicated agreement in paragraph 3 of the notice, he
will automatically be bound by your agreement, with effect from the date of
the transfer. Any subsequent landlord will also be bound.

Objection to being bound
2.   If the landlord has indicated an objection in paragraph 3 of the notice,
he will not be bound by your agreement unless *either* the landlord later
withdraws his objection *or* you apply to the County Court to declare that it
is reasonable for him to be bound, and the court so declares.

Validity of notice of objection
3.   A notice of objection by the landlord is only valid if he has given it to
each of you within the period of four weeks beginning with the date on which
you gave him your notice applying for your agreement to become binding
on him. If you are in any doubt, you should seek advice before applying to
the court.

FORM 8

PART I

JOINT NOTICE BY LANDLORD AND ASSIGNEE FOR BINDING APPORTIONMENT OF LIABILITY UNDER NON-ATTRIBUTABLE LANDLORD COVENANTS OF A TENANCY ON ASSIGNMENT OF PART OF REVERSION
(Landlord and Tenant (Covenants) Act 1995, sections 9 and 10)

To [name and address]: ....
....

IMPORTANT – THIS NOTICE IS INTENDED TO AFFECT THE WAY IN WHICH YOU CAN ENFORCE THE LANDLORD'S OBLIGATIONS UNDER THE TENANCY AS BETWEEN THE LANDLORD AND THE NEW LANDLORD. IF YOU CONSIDER THAT THERE IS GOOD REASON WHY YOU SHOULD **NOT** BE BOUND BY THEIR AGREEMENT, YOU MUST ACT QUICKLY. READ THE NOTICE AND ALL THE NOTES OVERLEAF CAREFULLY. IF YOU ARE IN ANY DOUBT ABOUT THE ACTION YOU SHOULD TAKE, SEEK ADVICE IMMEDIATELY, FOR INSTANCE FROM A SOLICITOR OR CITIZENS ADVICE BUREAU.

---

1. This notice is given under section 10 of the Landlord and Tenant (Covenants) Act 1995. *[see Note 1]*

2. It relates to (address and description of property) ....
....
let under a lease dated .... and made between ....
....
....
of which you are the tenant.

3. We are the parties to a [proposed transfer] [transfer on ....]¹ of the landlord's interest in part of the property comprised in the tenancy, namely ....
....
We are jointly and severally liable to perform the obligation(s) specified in the attached Schedule, and have agreed to divide that liability between us in

---

¹ Delete alternative as appropriate.

the manner specified in the Schedule.[2] We wish this agreement to be binding on you as well as between us, with effect from the date of the transfer. *[see Note 2]*

4. If you consider that it is reasonable for you to be bound by this agreement, you do not need to do anything, but it would help us if you notify us using Part II of this Form. *[see Note 3]*

5. If you do **not** consider it reasonable for you to be bound by this agreement, you **must** notify both of us of your objection, using Part II of this Form, within the period of **FOUR WEEKS** beginning with the giving of this notice. You may withdraw your objection at any time by notifying us in writing. *[see Notes 4–6]*

6. All correspondence about this notice should be copied, and one copy sent to each of the parties to the agreement, at the addresses given below.

Signature of landlord/landlord's agent ....
Name and address of landlord ....
....
....
[Name and address of agent ....
....
....]
Signature of new landlord/agent ....
Name and address of new landlord ....
....
....
[Name and address of agent ....
....
....]
Date ....

NOTES TO PART I

Apportionment of liability
1. The landlord is about to transfer, or has just transferred, part of his interest to a new landlord, but they are jointly and severally liable for a particular obligation or obligations covering the whole of the property. They

---

[2] The Schedule must be in writing, and must specify the nature of the obligation, the term or condition of the Lease or other instrument under which it arises and the manner in which liability to perform it is divided under the agreement. It may be helpful to attach a copy of the agreement to the notice.

have agreed to divide that liability between them, and are applying for you as tenant to be bound as well, so that you can only enforce the liability against each of them as set out in their agreement. If you are bound, any subsequent tenant to whom you may transfer your interest will also be bound. You have a number of options: you may expressly agree to be bound; you may object to being bound (with the option of withdrawing your objection later); or you may do nothing, in which case you will automatically be bound, with effect from the date of the transfer, once four weeks have elapsed from the date of the giving of the notice. If you choose to object, you must act within four weeks of the giving of the notice.

Validity of notice
2.   This notice must be given either before the transfer or within the period of four weeks beginning with the date of the transfer. If the notice has been given late, it is not valid. You should read Note 4 below concerning the date of the giving of the notice.

Agreeing to be bound
3.   If you are content to be bound, you may notify the landlord and new landlord using Part II of this Form (sending a copy to each of them), and all of you will be bound with effect from the date of the transfer. If you do this, you may not later change your mind and object.

Objecting to being bound
4.   If you think that it is not reasonable for you to be bound, you may object by notifying the landlord and new landlord, using Part II of this Form (sending a copy to each of them). You must, however, do this within four weeks of the date of the giving of the notice. The date of the giving of the notice may not be the date written on the notice or the date on which you actually saw it. It may, for instance, be the date on which the notice was delivered through the post to your last address known to the person giving the notice. If there has been any delay in your seeing this notice you may need to act very quickly. If you are in any doubt, you should seek advice immediately. If you change your mind after objecting, you may consent instead, at any time, by notifying *both* the landlord and new landlord *in writing* that you now consent to be bound and that your objection is withdrawn.

5.   If you object within the time limit, the apportionment will only bind you if *either* the landlord and new landlord apply to a court and the court decides that it is reasonable for you to be bound, *or* you withdraw your objection by notice in writing as explained in Note 4 above.

6.   In deciding whether to object, you should bear in mind that if the court finds that it is reasonable for you to be bound, *or* if you withdraw your objection late, you may have to pay costs.

PART II

TENANT'S RESPONSE TO JOINT NOTICE BY LANDLORD AND ASSIGNEE SEEKING BINDING APPORTIONMENT OF LIABILITY UNDER NON-ATTRIBUTABLE LANDLORD COVENANTS OF A TENANCY ON ASSIGNMENT OF PART OF REVERSION
(Landlord and Tenant (Covenants) Act 1995, section 10)

To [name and address]: ....

....

And [name and address]: ....

....

1. This notice is given under section 10 of the Landlord and Tenant (Covenants) Act 1995.

2. It relates to (address and description of property) ....

....

let under a lease dated .... and made between ....

....

....

of which I/we am/are the tenant.

3. You have applied for me/us to be bound by your agreement to divide liability between you with effect from the [proposed transfer] [transfer on ....]¹ of part of the landlord's interest in the property comprised in the tenancy.

4.² I/we agree to be bound by your agreement with effect from the date of the transfer. *[see Note 1]*

OR

4. I/we do **not** consider it reasonable that I/we should be bound by your agreement, and object to being so bound. *[see Notes 2 and 3]*

6. All correspondence about this notice should be sent to the tenant/tenant's agent at the address given below.

Date .... Signature of tenant/tenant's agent ....
Name and address of tenant ....

....

....

---

¹ Delete alternative as appropriate.
² The tenant should select one version of paragraph 4 and cross out the other.

[Name and address of agent ....

....

....]

NOTES TO PART II

Agreement to be bound
1.   If the tenant has indicated agreement in paragraph 3 of the notice, he will automatically be bound by your agreement, with effect from the date of the transfer. Any subsequent tenant will also be bound.

Objection to being bound
2.   If the tenant has indicated an objection in paragraph 3 of the notice, he will not be bound by your agreement unless *either* the tenant later withdraws his objection *or* you apply to the County Court to declare that it is reasonable for him to be bound, and the court so declares.

Validity of notice of objection
3.   A notice of objection by the tenant is only valid if he has given it to each of you within the period of four weeks beginning with the date on which you gave him your notice applying for your agreement to become binding on him. If you are in any doubt, you should seek advice before applying to the court.

EXPLANATORY NOTE

(This note is not part of the Regulations)

These Regulations prescribe the forms of notices to be used for the purposes of the Landlord and Tenant (Covenants) Act 1995. The forms are to be used for—

— notification by a landlord to a former tenant or guarantor who remains liable in respect of a covenant of the tenancy to pay a fixed charge, that sums for which he is liable under that covenant have become due and remain unpaid, and that the landlord intends to recover them from that person (Form 1);

— further notification by a landlord to a former tenant or guarantor, that a sum payable in respect of a fixed charge of which he has been given notice has now been determined to be greater than specified in the original notice, and that the landlord intends to recover that greater sum from that person (Form 2);

— a landlord's application for release from the covenants in the tenancy on assignment of his interest and for the tenant's response to this application (Form 3);

— a landlord's application for release from the covenants in the tenancy to the appropriate extent on assignment of part of his interest and for the tenant's response to this application (Form 4);

— a former landlord's application for release from the covenants in the tenancy on a subsequent assignment of the landlord's interest or part of it and for the tenant's response to this application (Form 5);

— a former landlord's application for release from the covenants in the tenancy to the appropriate extent on a subsequent assignment of the landlord's interest or part of it, where the former landlord assigned only part of the reversion, and for the tenant's response to this application (Form 6);

— an application by a tenant who assigns only part of his interest and the assignee to make an apportionment of their liability under certain covenants of the tenancy binding on the other party to the tenancy, and for the other party's response to this application (Form 7);

— an application by a landlord who assigns only part of his interest and the assignee to make an apportionment of their liability under certain covenants of the tenancy binding on the other party to the tenancy, and for the other party's response to this application (Form 8).

Reproductions or facsimiles of the notices may be used provided that they are substantially in the same form as prescribed in the Schedule to the regulations, including the notes.

Land Registration (No. 3) Rules 1995

SI 1995/3153

Made	*6th December 1995*
Laid before Parliament	*6th December 1995*
Coming into force	*1st January 1996*

The Lord Chancellor, with the advice and assistance of the Rule Committee appointed in pursuance of section 144 of the Land Registration Act 1925 **(a)**, in exercise of the powers conferred on him by that section and by section 38(2) of that Act **(b)**, hereby makes the following rules:

PART I   GENERAL

1.   Citation, commencement and interpretation

(1)   These rules may be cited as the Land Registration (No. 3) Rules 1995 and shall come into force on 1st January 1996.

(2)   In these rules:

(a)   'the principal rules' means the Land Registration Rules 1925 **(c)**;

(b)   a rule referred to by number means the rule so numbered in the principal rules.

PART II   DEFINITION OF 'PROPER OFFICES'

2.   Amendment to rule 1

The following paragraph is substituted for paragraph (5A) of rule 1:

'(5A) "Proper office" for the purposes of any application means the district registry within whose district, as constituted by orders made from time to time under section 132(1) of the Act, the land to which the application relates is situated or, where it is situated in the districts of two or more district registries, either or any of those district registries.'

3.   Revocation of Rules 24(4) and 83(2)

Rules 24(4)**(d)** and 83(2)**(e)** are revoked.

(a) 1925 c. 21; section 144(1) was amended by the Administration of Justice Act 1982 (c. 53), section 67(2) and Schedule 5, paragraph (d). The reference to the Ministry of Agriculture, Fisheries and Food was substituted by the Transfer of Functions (Ministry of Food) Order 1955 (SI 1955/554).
(b) Amended by the Law of Property (Miscellaneous Provisions) Act 1994 (c. 36), section 2(1) and Schedule 1 para. 2.
(c) SR & O 1925/1093; relevant amending instruments SI 1990/314, 1993/3275 and 1995/377.
(d) Added by SI 1990/314 rule 7.
(e) Inserted by SI 1990/314, rule 9.

4. Amendments to rules other than the principal rules

(1)   The definitions of 'proper office' in rule 1(2) of the Land Registration (Open Register) Rules 1991(**a**) and rule 2(1) of the Land Registration (Official Searches) Rules 1993(**b**) are revoked.

(2)   The following is substituted for the definition of 'proper office' in rule 2(1) of the Land Registration (Matrimonial Homes) Rules 1990(**c**):

"'proper office" has the meaning given to it by rule 1(5A) of the Land Registration Rules 1925(**d**).'

PART III   REGISTERED DEALINGS WITH REGISTERED LAND

5. Amendment to rule 1

In rule 1 the following paragraphs are inserted after paragraph (5J):

'(5K)   In these rules "new tenancy" has the same meaning as in section 1 of the Landlord and Tenant (Covenants) Act 1995(**e**), and "old tenancy" means a lease which is not a new tenancy.

(5L)   In these rules references to:

(a)   section 24 of the Act; or

(b)   section 77 of, or Schedule 2 to, the Law of Property Act 1925

as originally enacted,

are references to those provisions as they operate in relation to old tenancies by virtue of section 30(3) of the Landlord and Tenant (Covenants) Act 1995.'

6. Revocation of rule 76

Rule 76 is revoked.

7. New rule 109

(1)   The following rule is substituted for rule 109:

109.   'Transfer of land subject to a rentcharge

(1)   A transfer of land subject to a rentcharge not falling within paragraph (2) below shall be made by an instrument in Form 19 or 32.

(2)   A transfer of part of land subject to a rentcharge in which the rent is apportioned or land is exonerated from it shall be made by an instrument in Form 34B, or as near thereto as circumstances permit.

(3)   Where the convenants set out in Part VII or Part VIII of Schedule 2 to the Law of Property Act 1925(**f**) (in this rule called "the 1925 Act") are included in a transfer, the references to "the grantees",

(**a**) SI 1992/122.
(**b**) SI 1993/3276.
(**c**) 1990/1360.
(**d**) SR & O 1925/1093.
(**e**) 1995 c. 30.
(**f**) 15 Geo. 5 c. 20.

"the conveyance" and "the conveying parties" shall be treated as references to the transferees, the transfer and the transferors respectively.

(4) Where in a transfer part of land affected by a rentcharge is, without the consent of the owner of the rentcharge, expressed to be transferred exonerated from the entire rent, and the covenants in paragraph (ii) of Part VIII of Schedule 2 to the 1925 Act are included, that paragraph shall apply as if:

(a) any reference to the balance of the rent were to the entire rent; and

(b) the words ", other than the covenant to pay the entire rent," were omitted.

(5) Where in a transfer to which section 77(1)(B) of the 1925 Act does not apply part of land affected by a rentcharge is, without the consent of the owner of the rentcharge, expressed to be transferred subject to or charged with the entire rent, and the covenants in paragraph (i) of Part VIII of Schedule 2 to the 1925 Act are included, that paragraph shall apply as if:

(a) any reference to the apportioned rent were to the entire rent; and

(b) the words ", other than the covenant to pay the entire rent," were omitted.

(6) On a transfer of land subject to a rentcharge:

(a) any covenant implied by section 77(1)(A) or (B)(i) of the 1925 Act may be modified or negatived; and

(b) any covenant included in the instrument of transfer may be modified,

by adding suitable words to the instrument.'

(2) In the heading of Form 19 in the Schedule to the principal rules a reference to Rules 98 and 109 is substituted for the reference to Rule 98.

(3) The following note shall be inserted in the notes to Form 19 in the Schedule to the principal rules:

'(4A) Where the transfer is subject to a rentcharge (other than a rentcharge created after 22nd July 1977 by virtue of section 2(3)(a) or (b) of the Rentcharges Act 1977(**a**)) and no covenants are implied by section 77(1) of the Law of Property Act 1925(**b**), the appropriate covenants may be incorporated by adding the words "The covenants set out in Part VII (*or if the rent has previously been apportioned without the consent of the owner of the rentcharge,* paragraph (i) of Part VII) of Schedule 2 to the Law of Property Act 1925 shall be included in this transfer'.

(**a**) 1977 c. 30.
(**b**) 15 Geo. 5 c. 20.

8. New rules 115 and 116

The following rule is substituted for rule 115:

115. 'Transfer of leasehold land

(1) A transfer of leasehold land not falling within rule 116 shall be made by an instrument in Form 32 or 33.

(2) Where the transfer is a transfer of an old tenancy and covenants are to be implied under section 77 of the Law of Property Act 1925 as originally enacted, express reference shall be made in the transfer to that section.'

9. The following rule is substituted for rule 116:

116. 'Transfer of leasehold land, the rent being apportioned or land exonerated

(1) A transfer of part of leasehold land in which the rent is apportioned or land is exonerated from it shall be made by an instrument in Form 34 or 34A, or as near thereto as circumstances will permit.

(2) Where in a transfer part of land held under an old tenancy is, without the consent of the lessor, expressed to be transferred exonerated from the entire rent, and the covenants in paragraph (ii) of Part X of Schedule 2 to the Law of Property Act 1925 as originally enacted are included, that paragraph shall apply as if:

(a) any reference to the balance of the rent were to the entire rent; and

(b) the words '', other than the covenant to pay the entire rent,'' were omitted.

(3) Where in a transfer to which section 77(1)(D) of the Law of Property Act 1925 as originally enacted does not apply part of land held under an old tenancy is, without the consent of the lessor, expressed to be transferred subject to or charged with the entire rent, and the covenants in paragraph (i) of Part X of Schedule 2 to the Law of Property Act 1925 as originally enacted are included, that paragraph shall apply as if:

(a) any reference to the apportioned rent were to the entire rent; and

(b) the words '', other than the covenant to pay the entire rent,'' were omitted.

(4) Where the transfer is a transfer of part of the land held under an old tenancy and covenants are to be implied under section 24 of the Act, express reference shall be made in the transfer to that section.'

10. New rule 117

The following rule is substituted for rule 117:

117. 'Variation of implied covenants in transfer of land held under old tenancy

(1) Where in a transfer the covenants set out in Part IX or Part X of Schedule 2 to the Law of Property Act 1925 as originally enacted are included, the references to "the assignees", "the conveyance" and "the conveying parties" shall be treated as references to the transferees, the transfer and the transferors respectively.

(2) On a transfer of land held under an old tenancy:

(a) any covenants implied by section 24 of the Act or by section 77(1)(C) or (D)(i) of the Law of Property Act 1925 as originally enacted may be modified or negatived; and

(b) any covenants included in the instrument of transfer may be modified

by adding suitable words to the instrument, and a note shall be made in the register.'

11. New Forms 32, 33, 34, 34A and 34B

Forms 32, 33, 34, 34A and 34B in the Schedule to these rules shall be substituted for Forms 32, 33 and 34 in the Schedule to the principal rules.

Dated 6th December   *Mackay of Clashfern*, C.

SCHEDULE
FORM 32

TRANSFER OF LEASEHOLD LAND (WHOLE OR PART)
(Rules 109 and 115)

As Form 19 or Form 20, adding at the end 'for the residue of the term granted by the registered lease.'

Where it is intended to negative the covenants implied by Section 24 of the Act in relation to the transfer of an old tenancy, the following words may be added to the form:

'The covenant by the transferor (*or* transferee, *or* the covenants by the transferor and transferee) implied by Section 24 of the Act is (*or* are) not to be implied.'

FORM 33

TRANSFER OF LEASEHOLD LAND (WHOLE) BEING PART OF THE LAND ORIGINALLY COMPRISED IN THE LEASE, WHERE THE RENT HAS ALREADY BEEN APPORTIONED
(Rule 115)

(*Date.*) In consideration of   pounds (£   ), I, A.B., of &c., transfer to C. D., of &c., the land comprised in the title above referred to for the residue of the term granted by the registered lease subject to the apportioned rent of £   being part of the rent of £   reserved by the registered lease.

Note.—Where it is intended to negative the covenants implied by section 24 of the Act in relation to the transfer of an old tenancy, the following words may be added to the form:

'The covenant by the transferee implied by section 24 of the Act is not to be implied.'

FORM 34

TRANSFER OF LAND HELD UNDER A NEW TENANCY (PART), IN WHICH RENT IS APPORTIONED OR LAND EXONERATED
(Rule 116)
(Heading as in Form 19)

(*Date.*) In consideration of   pounds (£   ), A.B., of &c., transfer to C. D., of &c., the land shown and edged with red on the accompanying plan, being part of the land comprised in the title above referred to for the residue of the term granted by the registered lease.

It is agreed that liability for the payment of [*where rent previously apportioned* the previously apportioned rent of £   being part of] the rent reserved by the registered lease is apportioned between the parties as follows:

£   (*or* The whole) shall be payable out of the land hereby transferred

The balance of £   (*or* The whole) shall be payable out of the residue of the land in the title(s) above referred to

If the whole rent is to be payable by one party, omit whichever of the above does not apply and add, and the residue of the land in the title(s) above referred to (*or* the land hereby transferred *as the case may be*) is exonerated from the said rent.

(To be executed as Form 19 by both parties)

FORM 34A

TRANSFER OF LAND HELD UNDER AN OLD TENANCY (PART), IN WHICH THE RENT IS APPORTIONED OR LAND EXONERATED
(Rule 116)

As Form 34, adding if desired, where the rent is apportioned or land exonerated without the consent of the lessor, 'The covenants set out in paragraph (ii) of Part X of Schedule 2 to the Law of Property Act 1925 shall be included in this transfer.'

The covenants set out in paragraph (i) of the said Part X may, where no covenants are implied by section 77(1)(D)(i) of the Law of Property Act 1925 as originally enacted, be incorporated by omitting the words 'paragraph (ii) of'.

Mutual charges in support of the covenants may be added if desired, and if added should be accompanied by application to register notice thereof.

Where the rent is apportioned or land exonerated with the consent of the lessor and no covenants are implied by section 77(1)(c) of the Law of Property Act 1925 as originally enacted, the appropriate covenants may be incorporated by adding the words, 'The covenants set out in Part IX of Schedule 2 to the Law of Property Act 1925 shall be included in this transfer.'

FORM 34B

TRANSFER OF LAND SUBJECT TO A RENTCHARGE (PART), IN WHICH THE RENT IS APPORTIONED OR LAND EXONERATED
(Rule 109)
(Heading as in Form 19)

(*Date.*) In consideration of   pounds (£   ), A.B., of &c., hereby transfers to C. D., of &c., the land shown and edged with red on the accompanying plan, being part of the land comprised in the title above referred to.

It is agreed that liability for the payment of [*where rent previously apportioned* the previously apportioned rent of £   being part of] the yearly rentcharge of £   created by (*describe instrument*) to which the land transferred with other land is subject, is apportioned between the parties as follows:

£   (*or* The whole) shall be payable out of the land hereby transferred

The balance of £   (*or* The whole) shall be payable out of the residue of the land in the title(s) above referred to

If the whole rent is to be payable by one party, omit whichever of the above does not apply and add, and the residue of the land in the title(s) above referred to (*or* the land hereby transferred *as the case may be*) is exonerated from the said rent.

If the rent is apportioned or land exonerated without the consent of the owner of the rentcharge add, if desired: The covenants set out in paragraph (ii) of Part VIII of Schedule 2 to the Law of Property Act 1925 shall be included in this transfer.

(To be executed as Form 19 by both parties)

Note.—The covenants set out in paragraph (i) of the said Part VIII may, where no covenants are implied by section 77(1)(B)(i) of the Law of Property Act 1925, be included by omitting the words 'paragraph (ii) of'.

Mutual charges in support of the covenants may be added if desired, and if added should be accompanied by application to register notice thereof.

Where the rent is apportioned or land exonerated with the consent of the owner of the rentcharge and no covenants are implied by section 77(1)(A) of the Law of Property Act 1925, the appropriate covenants may be incorporated by adding the words, 'The covenants set out in Part VII of Schedule 2 to the Law of Property Act 1925 shall be included in this transfer.'

EXPLANATORY NOTE

(This note does not form part of the Rules)

These Rules, which come into force on 1 January 1996, amend the Land Registration Rules 1925 ('the 1925 Rules'), the Land Registration (Matrimonial Homes) Rules 1990, the Land Registration (Open Register) Rules 1991 and the Land Registration (Official Searches) Rules 1993.

'Proper office' is defined in rule 1(5A) of the 1925 Rules for the purposes of all four of these sets of rules. The proper office is the district registry within whose district the land, or any of the land, to which an application relates is situated.

New rules are substituted for rules 115 and 116 of the 1925 Rules to provide for transfers of land held under 'new tenancies' within the meaning of the Landlord and Tenant (Covenants) Act 1995 (that is, leases granted on or after 1 January 1996 otherwise than in pursuance of an agreement entered into, an option granted or a court order made before that date) as well as transfers of land held under leases which are not new tenancies.

The covenants implied by section 24 of the Land Registration Act 1925 and Section 77 of the Law of Property Act 1925 as originally enacted, both repealed in relation to new tenancies, can only apply to transfers of land held under leases which are not new tenancies. This is reflected in the new rules.

Rule 76 of the 1925 Rules, which provided for land subject to a rentcharge and leasehold land to be transferred as beneficial owner, etc. so as to imply the covenants by the transferor implied by section 77 of the Law of Property Act 1925, is revoked. New rules and forms allow the appropriate covenants to be incorporated in transfers without the transfer being made as beneficial owner.

New rule 109 (Transfers of land subject to a rentcharge) adapts the wording of Parts VII and VIII of Schedule 2 to the Law of Property Act 1925 to the requirements of registered conveyancing. It applies to transfers of either freehold or leasehold land.

A new rule 117 (Variation of implied covenants in transfer of land held under old tenancy) adapts the wording of Parts IX and X of Schedule 2 (saved in relation to leases which are not new tenancies) to the requirements of registered conveyancing, and provides for a note to be made on the register when the implied covenants are modified or negatived.

New Forms 32, 33, 34, 34A and 34B are substituted for Forms 32, 33 and 34 in the Schedule to the 1925 Rules.

Land Registration (Overriding Leases) Rules 1995

Made	*6th December 1995*
Laid before Parliament	*6th December 1995*
Coming into force	*1st January 1996*

The Lord Chancellor, with the advice and assistance of the Rule Committee appointed in pursuance of section 144 of the Land Registration Act 1925(**a**), in exercise of the powers conferred on him by that section and by section 20(2) of the Landlord and Tenant (Covenants) Act 1995(**b**), hereby makes the following rules:

1. Citation and commencement

These rules may be cited as the Land Registration (Overriding Leases) Rules 1995 and shall come into force on 1st January 1996.

2. Statement to be inserted in an overriding lease

The statement required by section 20(2) of the Landlord and Tenant (Covenants) Act 1995 to be inserted into an overriding lease granted under section 19 of that Act shall in relation to a registrable lease be in the following form:

'This lease is granted under section 19 of the Landlord and Tenant (Covenants) Act 1995 and is (*or* is not) a new tenancy for the purposes of section 1 of that Act.'

Dated 6th December 1995   *Mackay of Clashfern, C.*

(**a**) 1925 c. 21; section 144(1) was amended by the Administration of Justice Act 1982 (c. 53), section 67(2) and Schedule 5, paragraph (d). The reference to the Ministry of Agriculture, Fisheries and Food was substituted by the Transfer of Functions (Ministry of Food) Order 1955 (SI 1955/554).
(**b**) 1995 c. 30.

EXPLANATORY NOTE

(This note does not form part of the rules.)

These rules, which come into force on 1st January 1996, prescribe the statement required by section 20(2) of the Landlord and Tenant (Covenants) Act 1995 to be inserted into an overriding lease granted under section 19 of that Act.

Appendix 4

Precedents

Framework for a commercial lease*

LEASE: DATED

1 *PARTICULARS*

1.1 LANDLORD:

1.2 TENANT:

1.3 GUARANTOR:

1.4 PREMISES: ALL THAT   shown for the purpose of identification only edged red on the plan annexed hereto ('the Plan')

1.5 CONTRACTUAL TERM: years commencing on the day of 199

1.6 RENT COMMENCEMENT DATE: The   day of   199

1.7 RENT: £ (pounds) per year

1.8 INTEREST RATE: per year above the base lending rate of or such other bank (being a member of the Committee of London and Scottish Bankers) as the Landlord may from time to time nominate in writing and 'Interest' means interest during the period from the date on which payment is due to the date of payment both before and after any judgment at the Interest Rate then prevailing from time to time or (should the base lending rate referred to above cease to exist) such other rate of interest as is most closely comparable with the Interest Rate to be agreed between the parties or in default of agreement to be determined by the Landlord's Surveyor acting as an expert and not as an arbitrator

1.9 PERMITTED USE: Use as   within Class   of the Town and Country Planning (Use Classes) Order 1987 (notwithstanding any amendment or revocation of such Order)

---

* Note common form clauses have not been reproduced in full.

1.10 EXTERIOR DECORATING YEAR(S): The [and] last year(s) of the Term

1.11 INTERIOR DECORATING YEAR(S): The [and] last year(s) of the Term

2 DEFINITIONS AND INTERPRETATION

2.1 Unless the context otherwise requires, in this lease the expressions defined in clauses 1 and 2 hereof shall have the meanings given to them in the definitions in those clauses.

2.2 'Authorised Guarantee Agreement' means an agreement in the form set out in the Fourth Schedule hereto

2.3 'Building' means the building or buildings now or at any time during the Term standing on the whole or part of the Premises

2.4 'Conducting Media' means all pipes sewers drains mains ducts conduits gutters watercourses wires cables channels flues and all other conducting media and includes any fixings louvres cowls and other ancillary apparatus

2.5 'Development' has the meaning given by section 55 of the Town and Country Planning Act 1990

2.6 'Guarantor' includes not only the person referred to in clause 1.3 (if any) but also any person who enters into covenants with the Landlord pursuant to any provision in this Lease

2.7 'Insurance Rent' means the costs and expenses from time to time incurred by the Landlord under clause 5.2 of this Lease

2.8 'Insured Risks' means the risks of fire explosion flood storm tempest impact riot civil commotion aircraft or other aerial devices and articles dropped therefrom and such other risks as the Landlord shall from time to time deem it prudent to insure against

2.9 'Landlord' includes where the context so admits that person from time to time entitled to the reversion immediately expectant on the determination of the Term

2.10 'Particulars' means the description and terms appearing under the heading 'Particulars' in this Lease and the Particulars are deemed to comprise part of this Lease

2.11 'Planning Act' means the Town and Country Planning Act 1990

2.12 'Premises' includes

(a)   the Building

(b)   all additions and improvements to the Premises

(c)   all the Landlord's fixtures and fittings and all other fixtures of every kind which shall from time to time be in or upon the Premises (whether originally affixed or fastened to or upon the Premises or otherwise) except any trade fixtures installed by the Tenant which can be removed from the Premises without causing any damage to the Premises

(d)   all Conducting Media in on under or over the Premises and

(e)   all (if any) walls and fences forming the boundaries of the Premises but 'Premises' include no air space above or surrounding the Premises as they are at the date of this Lease and references to 'Premises' in the absence of any indication to the contrary include references to each and any part of the Premises

2.13   'Rents' means the rents firstly and thirdly reserved in clause 3 and the Insurance Rent and shall also include any rent the amount of which is determined by the court under section 24A of the 1954 Act

2.14   'Tenant' includes where the context so admits the Tenant's successors in title

2.15   'Term' means the Contractual Term and any period of holding-over or extension or continuance of the Contractual Term whether by statute or common law

2.16   'Terminating Event' means any of the following

(a)   in relation to an individual

(i)   the making of an application for the appointment of an interim receiver in respect of the individual under section 286 of the Insolvency Act 1986

(ii)   the making of a bankruptcy order in respect of the individual

(iii) the making of an application for an interim order under section 253 of the Insolvency Act 1986

(iv) the appointment of any person by the court to prepare a report under section 273 of the Insolvency Act 1986 in respect of the individual

(b)   in relation to a company:

(i)   the making of an administration order in respect of the company or the presentation of a petition for such an order

(ii)   any person becoming entitled to exercise in relation to thcompany the powers conferred on an administrative receiver

(iii) the making of an order or the passing of a resolution to wind up the company

(iv) the appointment of a provisional liquidator in respect of the company

(v)   the making of a proposal under section 1 of the Insolvency Act 1986 for a voluntary arrangement in respect of the company

(vi)   the making of a return or reduction of capital

(c)   in relation to any person (whether an individual or a company)

(i)   the appointment of a receiver (including an administrative receiver) in respect of any of the person's assets

(ii)   the person entering into an arrangement for the benefit of creditors

(iii)   any distress or execution being levied (except by or on behalf of the Landlord) on any of the person's assets

(iv)   that person ceases for any reason to be or remain liable to perform its obligations contained in this Lease

2.17   '1954 Act' means the Landlord and Tenant Act 1954

2.18   If at any time the Landlord the Tenant or any Guarantor comprises two or more persons obligations expressed or implied to be made by the Landlord the Tenant or the Guarantor as the case may be are deemed to be made by such persons jointly and severally

2.19   Words importing one gender include all other genders and words importing the singular include the plural and vice versa

2.20   Any reference to 'the last year of the Term' includes reference to the last year of the Term if the Term shall determine otherwise than by effluxion of time and any reference to 'the expiration of the Term' includes reference to such other determination of the Term

2.21   References to any right of the Landlord to have access to the Premises shall be construed as extending to all persons authorised by the Landlord to enjoy such access (including agents professional advisers contractors and workmen)

2.22   Any covenant by the Tenant not to do an act or thing shall be deemed to include an obligation not to permit or suffer such act or thing to be done by another person

2.23   References to 'consent of the Landlord' or words to similar effect refer to a consent in writing signed by or on behalf of the Landlord and 'approved' 'authorised' or words to similar effect mean (as the case may be) approved or authorised in writing by or on behalf of the Landlord

2.24   The term 'parties' or 'party' mean the Landlord and/or the Tenant but except where there is an express indication to the contrary exclude any Guarantor

2.25   Any reference (whether specific or general) to any statute or statutes includes reference to any statutory extension modification amendment or re-enactment of and any subordinate legislation made under such statute or statutes

2.26   References in this Lease to clauses sub-clauses or schedules shall be construed as references to the clauses sub-clauses or schedules of this Lease so numbered and/or lettered unless otherwise expressly specified

2.27   The clause paragraph and schedule headings do not form part of this Lease and shall not be taken into account in its construction or interpretation

3   *DEMISE AND RENTS*

THE Landlord LETS to the Tenant the Premises TOGETHER WITH the easements and other rights mentioned in the First Schedule EXCEPT AND RESERVING as mentioned in the Second Schedule SUBJECT to the matters mentioned in the Third Schedule and to all other rights easements quasi-easements and privileges to which the Premises are subject for the term of   years from   YIELDING AND PAYING the following rents clear of all deductions whatsoever

FIRST the YEARLY RENT of   to be paid by bankers order (if the Landlord so requires) in advance by equal quarterly payments on the usual quarter days the first of such payments in respect of the period from the   to the next quarter day to be made on   19

SECONDLY on demand the Insurance Rent

THIRDLY on demand all expenses which the Landlord may from time to time incur in connection with or in procuring the remedying of any breach of the Tenant's covenants contained in this Lease

4   *TENANT'S COVENANTS*

The Tenant COVENANTS throughout the Term

4.1   To pay the Rents

4.2   To pay Interest

4.3   To pay all existing and future rates etc.

4.4   To pay value added tax

4.5   To keep the Premises in good and substantial repair

[4.6, 4.7   Further repair/insurance covenants]

4.8   To paint the Premises in colours first approved by the Landlord in a good and workmanlike manner externally in the Exterior Decorating Year(s) and internally in the Interior Decorating Year(s)

4.9   To keep the Premises in a clean and tidy condition

4.10   To permit the Landlord to inspect

4.11   Not to use the Premises for any noisy noisome offensive dangerous illegal or immoral purpose [etc.]

4.12   Not to use the Premises otherwise than for the Permitted Use

4.13   To comply with all conditions in any planning permission relating to the Premises

4.14   Not to make or permit or suffer any structural alterations or additions to the Premises whatsoever and not to make or permit or suffer any other alterations or additions except with the prior written consent of the Landlord

4.15   *Alienation*
   (a)   Not to mortgage charge or grant any security interest over the whole or any part of the Premises nor to assign any part of the Premises nor except as permitted under (d) of this clause to share or part with the possession or occupation of the whole or any part of the Premises
   (b)   Not to assign the whole of the Premises without the consent of the Landlord such consent not to be unreasonably withheld provided that the Landlord may withhold its consent to assignment in the following circumstances
      (i)   if the Tenant shall fail to provide to the Landlord such information and references as the Landlord shall [reasonably] require
      (ii)   if there are any outstanding breaches of the Tenant's obligations under this Lease
      (iii)   [insert such other conditions as may be appropriate]
   (c)   Conditions subject to which any licence to assign shall be given are
      (i)   that any intended assignee shall covenant with the Landlord to pay the rent reserved by and observe and perform the covenants and conditions on the part of the Tenant contained in this Lease
      (ii)   that such persons as the Landlord may require shall act as guarantors for an intended assignee in such form as the Landlord may require
      (iii)   that the Tenant shall enter into an Authorised Guarantee Agreement
   (d)   If the Tenant shall desire to underlet or agree to underlet the whole or any part of the Premises and shall procure
      (i)   that any intended underlessee shall covenant with the Landlord to observe and perform the covenants and conditions on the part of the Tenant herein contained (excluding the covenant to pay Rents) and not further to underlet assign share or part with possession or occupation of the whole or part of the premises to be so underlet

(ii)   that no underlease shall be granted at a premium or at a rent less than the greater of a rack rent for the underlet premises and the rent FIRST reserved (or a proportion thereof in the case of an underletting of part of the Premises) at the time of the underletting and payable no more than one quarter in advance

(iii)   that any underlease of part of the Premises shall contain an agreement authorised by the court to exclude the provisions of sections 24 to 28 of the Landlord and Tenant Act 1954
then the Tenant may underlet the whole or any approved part of the Premises with the prior written consent of the Landlord

4.16   Registration of dealings with Landlord

4.17   To reimburse the Landlord on demand all costs incurred

(a)   in connection with or in contemplation of the preparation and service of a notice and/or any proceedings under section 146 or section 147 of the Law of Property Act 1925 or under the Leasehold Property (Repairs) Act 1938 (notwithstanding that forfeiture is avoided)

(b)   in connection with or in contemplation of the preparation and service of a schedule of dilapidations at any time during or after termination of the Term (but relating only to dilapidations which accrued prior to the termination of the Term)

(c)   in connection with the preparation and completion of this Lease

(d)   in connection with any applications for consent or approval including cases where consent or approval is refused or the application is withdrawn

4.18   To permit the Landlord to fix on the Premises a noticeboard for the reletting or the sale of the Premises

4.19   To indemnify Landlord

4.20   To yield up

4.21   To perform and observe the covenants agreements and stipulations contained or referred to in the documents listed in the Third Schedule insofar as they relate to the Premises or the rights hereby granted

5   LANDLORD'S COVENANTS

The Landlord HEREBY COVENANTS with the Tenant subject to the Tenant paying the Rents hereby reserved and observing and performing all covenants and the conditions in this Lease

5.1   Quiet enjoyment

5.2   To insure

5.3   To rebuild

6.1   *Forfeiture*
If and whenever during the Term
   (a)   the Rents or any other sum due under this Lease shall be in arrear for fourteen days (in the case of the rent firstly reserved in clause 3 whether formally demanded or not) or
   (b)   the Tenant shall fail to observe or perform any of its covenants and the conditions in this Lease or in any document supplemental to this Lease or
   (c)   there is a breach by any Guarantor of the Guarantor's covenants contained in this Lease or of any covenants in favour of the Landlord entered into by any new additional substitute or other guarantor of any other person (whether an assignee or underlessee or otherwise) (a 'Covenantor') pursuant to this Lease or
   (d)   there occurs in relation to the Tenant or any Guarantor (or where the Tenant or any Guarantor comprises two or more persons there occurs in relation to any of such persons) or a Covenantor a Terminating Event or
   (e)   any Guarantor who is an individual (or where any Guarantor comprises two or more persons any of such persons being an individual) dies or has a receiver appointed under the Mental Health Act 1983
then and in any such case the Landlord may forfeit this Lease but without prejudice to any other remedy of the Landlord in respect of any antecedent breach of any of the covenants or conditions contained in this Lease

6.2   Nothing in this Lease shall confer upon the Tenant any easement right or privilege whatsoever over or against any land adjoining or neighbouring the Premises which now or hereafter shall belong to the Landlord save as expressly hereby granted or impose any restriction on the use of any land not comprised in this Lease

6.3   The right of the Tenant (or any undertenant) to compensation on quitting the Premises is excluded

6.4   *Cesser of rent*
If the Premises shall be damaged or destroyed by any of the insured risks so as to be unfit for occupation and use in accordance with this Lease then (unless the insurance money shall be wholly or partially irrecoverable by reason solely or in part of any act or default of the Tenant or any person deriving title under the Tenant or any of the Tenant's servants agents or licensees) the rent firstly reserved in clause 3 or a fair proportion (determined by the Landlord) according to the nature and extent of the damage shall be suspended until the Premises shall again be fit for occupation and use or (if earlier) the expiry of   years

6.5 *Notices*

Section 196 of the Law of Property Act 1925 (as amended) shall be deemed to be incorporated herein

7.1 *GUARANTEE*

THE Guarantor COVENANTS with the Landlord that

(a) the Tenant will pay the rents reserved and observe and perform its covenants and conditions in this Lease and the Guarantor will indemnify the Landlord on demand against all losses damages costs and expenses arising out of any default by the Tenant

(b) if for any reason the Term shall be prematurely determined or a liquidator or trustee in bankruptcy of the Tenant disclaims this Lease or if this Lease shall otherwise be disclaimed in circumstances releasing the estate of the Tenant from liability or if this lease is determined by forfeiture or re-entry and if within six months of any such event the Landlord shall by notice in writing so require the Guarantor will enter into a new lease of the Premises at the cost of the Guarantor on the same terms for the residue of the Term which would have remained had there been no such determination disclaimer forfeiture or re-entry

(c) if the Landlord does not require the Guarantor to take a new lease pursuant to sub-clause 7.1(b) above the Guarantor will pay to the Landlord on demand a sum equal to the Rents and other moneys that would have been payable under this Lease but for such determination disclaimer forfeiture or re-entry until the expiration of six months therefrom or until the Premises shall have been relet whichever shall first occur

7.2 The liability of the Guarantor hereunder shall not be affected by any neglect or forbearance of the Landlord in enforcing the payment of the Rents or the observance or performance of the said covenants and conditions or any refusal by the Landlord to accept rent at a time when the Landlord was entitled (or would after the service of a notice under section 146 of the Law of Property Act 1925 have been entitled) to re-enter the Premises or any variation of the terms of this Lease or any change in the constitution structure or powers of the Guarantor the Tenant or the Landlord or any act which is beyond the powers of the Tenant or the surrender of part of the Premises

7.3 As between the Landlord and the Guarantor the Guarantor shall be deemed to be a principal debtor

7.4 The Guarantor shall not be entitled to participate in any security held by the Landlord in respect of the Tenant's obligations or stand in the Landlord's place in respect of such security

7.5   Where the Guarantor is more than one person the release of one or more of them shall not release the others

[8   *STAMP DUTY CERTIFICATE*

The Landlord and the Tenant hereby certify that there is no agreement for lease to which this Lease gives effect]

IN WITNESS whereof this Lease has been executed as a deed by the parties hereto the day and year first before written

FIRST SCHEDULE
Rights granted

The right for the Tenant and all persons authorised by the Tenant (including contractors and workmen) to enter the air space above and surrounding the Premises but so far only as such entry may be

(a)   necessary to enable the Tenant to perform its obligations under this Lease or any document supplemental to this Lease or

(b)   reasonably incidental to the use and enjoyment of the Premises in accordance with the terms of this Lease

SECOND SCHEDULE
Rights reserved

The right at any time during the Term at reasonable times and upon reasonable notice except in cases of emergency to enter (or in cases of emergency to break and enter) the Premises

(a)   to inspect the condition and state of repair of the Premises

(b)   to take schedules or inventories of fixtures and other items to be yielded up on the expiry of the Term and

(c)   to exercise any of the rights granted to the Landlord elsewhere in this Lease

THIRD SCHEDULE
Documents which affect or relate to the Premises

FOURTH SCHEDULE
Authorised Guarantee Agreement

The Tenant covenants with the Landlord that

(a)   the Assignee [*there may be inserted here* 'until released from liability under the terms of the Landlord and Tenant (Covenants) Act 1995'. *These words are unnecessary as the release of the guarantor on that event is automatic (s. 24(2)). Without these words the agreement is a valid AGA 'to the extent' that it is permitted by s. 16(4), i.e. until such release]* will pay the Rents reserved and observe and perform its covenants and conditions in this Lease and the Tenant will indemnify the Landlord on demand against all losses damages costs and expenses arising out of any default by the Assignee

(b)   if for any reason the Term shall be prematurely determined or liquidated or a trustee in bankruptcy of the Assignee disclaims this Lease or if this Lease shall otherwise be disclaimed in circumstances releasing the estate of the Assignee from liability or if this Lease is determined by forfeiture or re-entry and if within six months of any such event the Landlord shall by notice in writing so require the Tenant will enter into a new lease of the Premises at the cost of the Tenant on the same terms for the residue of the term which would have remained had there been no such determination, disclaimer, forfeiture or re-entry

(c)   if the Landlord does not require the Tenant to take a new lease pursuant to sub-clause (b) above the Tenant will pay to the Landlord on demand a sum equal to the Rents and other moneys that would have been payable under this Lease but for such determination disclaimer forfeiture or re-entry until the expiration of six months therefrom or until the premises shall have been re-let whichever shall first occur

2   The liability of the Tenant hereunder shall not be affected by any neglect or forbearance of the Landlord in enforcing the payments of the Rents or the observance or performance of the said covenants and conditions or any refusal by the Landlord to accept rent at a time when the Landlord was entitled (or would after service of a notice under section 46 of the Law of Property Act 1925 have been entitled) to re-enter the premises or any variation of the terms of this Lease or any change in the constitution structure or powers of the Tenant the Assignee or the Landlord or any act which is beyond the powers of the Assignee or the surrender of part of the premises

3   As between the Landlord and the Tenant the Tenant shall be deemed to be a principal debtor

4   The Tenant shall not be entitled to participate in any security held by the Landlord in respect of the Assignee's obligations or stand in the Landlord's place in respect of such security

5   Where the Tenant is more than one person the release of one or more of them shall not release the others

THE COMMON SEAL of
was hereunto affixed in the presence of

      Director

      Secretary

SIGNED as a deed by the said
in the presence of
Witness
Address

Occupation

Overriding lease

[LEASE DATED   ]

[HM LAND REGISTRY
LAND REGISTRATION ACTS 1925 to 1986
LEASE OF WHOLE

[County and district or
London borough]
Title number
Property
Date   ]

1   In this lease the following expressions have the following meanings:

1.1	the Landlord	[insert name and address]
1.2	the Tenant	[insert name and address]
1.3	the Original Lease	[insert details]
1.4	the Original Tenant	[insert name and address]
1.5	the Original Landlord	[insert name and address]
1.6	the Premises	the premises demised by the Original Lease
1.7	the Term	the residue now unexpired at the date of this Lease of the term granted by the Original Lease plus three days
1.8	the Act	the Landlord and Tenant (Covenants) Act 1995
1.9	the Payment	the sum payable by the Tenant to the Landlord under section 17 of the Act
1.10	the Rent	the rent payable under the Original Lease

2.   This lease is an overriding lease granted under section 19 of the Act and is [or is not] a new tenancy for the purposes of section 1 of the Act.*

3   In consideration of the Payment made by the Tenant to the Landlord (receipt of which the Landlord acknowledges) and of the rent and covenants contained below the Landlord demises to the Tenant the Premises together

---

* This statement is required by s. 20(2) of the 1995 Act and is prescribed by the Land Registration (Overriding Leases) Rules 1995 (see appendix 3).

with the rights granted to the Original Tenant by the Original Lease and subject to but with the benefit of the original Lease TO HOLD to the Tenant for the Term YIELDING AND PAYING to the Landlord the Rent in accordance with the terms for payment in the Original Lease

4   The Tenant covenants with the Landlord

4.1   to observe and perform all the covenants and conditions on the part of the Original Tenant contained in the Original Lease except those set out in the Schedule hereto

4.2   to pay the Landlord's solicitors' and surveyors' fees in connection with the negotiation preparation execution and grant of this lease

5   The Landlord covenants with the Tenant to observe and perform all the covenants and conditions on the part of the Original Landlord contained in the Original Lease

6   Provided always and it is agreed as follows that

(a)   if the time for complying with any covenant in the Original Lease is calculated by reference to the commencement of the term granted by the Original Lease then the time for complying with that covenant shall be the same under this Lease

(b)   if the rent or any part of it is in arrear for 21 days after becoming payable or there is any breach of any of the Tenant's covenants or if the Tenant is adjudicated bankrupt or (being a company) goes into liquidation otherwise than for the purpose of amalgamation or reconstruction then in any such event the Landlord may re-enter the Premises or any part of them in the name of the whole and thereupon this lease shall absolutely determine

7   The Landlord and the Tenant hereby verify that there is no agreement for lease to which this Lease gives effect

IN WITNESS whereof this Lease has been executed as a deed by the parties
hereto the day and the year first before written

THE SCHEDULE
Covenants in the Original Lease which do not apply

[Insert details of spent or personal covenants]

THE COMMON SEAL of
was hereunto affixed in the presence of

      Director

      Secretary

SIGNED as a deed by the said
in the presence of
Witness
Address

Occupation

Alienation clauses

Precedent 1

Not to assign underlet charge part with possession of or share possession or occupation of the whole of the Premises without the prior written consent of the Landlord such consent not to be unreasonably withheld provided always in the case of an assignment that if [any of] the following conditions[s] [is] [are] not fulfilled it shall not be unreasonable for the Landlord to withhold such consent

(a)   The Assignee did not have net profits before taxation in [his] [its] last accounts of at least [three] times the Rent and for the purposes of this clause the assignee is required to have [his] [its] accounts audited at [his] [its] own expense, if not already audited

(b)   On an assignment to a limited company the Assignee must procure that at least two directors of the company or some other person or persons reasonably acceptable to the Landlord enter into direct covenants with the Landlord [in the form of the covenants contained in clause [X] of this Lease] [with 'the Assignee' substituted for 'the Tenant'] [or] [in such form as shall be [reasonably] specified at that time by the Landlord]

(c)   On an assignment to an individual the Assignee must procure that some other person or persons reasonably acceptable to the Landlord enter into direct covenants with the Landlord [in the form of the covenants contained in clause [X] of this Lease [with 'the Assignee' substituted for 'the Tenant'] [or] [in such form as shall be [reasonably] specified at that time by the Landlord]

(d)   In the reasonable opinion of the Landlord the Assignee is in competition with the business of [the Landlord] [another tenant in the building]

(e)   In the opinion of the Landlord the Assignee is not of equal financial status to the Tenant provided that if the Tenant does not agree with the opinion of the Landlord the matter may if the Tenant so chooses be determined by an independent third party to be appointed by agreement between the parties or (in the absence of agreement) nominated by the [President of the Law Society] [President of the Royal Institution of Chartered Surveyors] (or his nominee) on the application of the Tenant made within four weeks of the date on which the Landlord notifies the Tenant of his decision

(f)   All the covenants contained in this Lease on the part of the Tenant have been fully complied with

(g)   Any outstanding rent review under this Lease has been completed

Precedent 2

The Landlord's consent shall be given subject to the following conditions:

(a)   That the Tenant shall enter into an agreement with the Landlord in which he covenants with the Landlord that:

(i)   (1)   the Assignee while tenant will pay the Rents reserved and observe and perform its covenants and conditions in this Lease and the Tenant will indemnify the Landlord on demand against all losses damages costs and expenses arising out of any default by the Assignee

(2)   if for any reason the Term shall be prematurely determined or liquidated or a trustee in bankruptcy of the Assignee disclaims this Lease or if this Lease shall otherwise be disclaimed in circumstances releasing the estate of the Assignee from liability or if this Lease is determined by forfeiture or re-entry and if within six months of any such event the Landlord shall by notice in writing so require the Tenant will enter into a new lease of the Premises at the cost of the Tenant on the same terms for the residue of the term which would have remained had there been no such determination disclaimer forfeiture or re-entry

(3)   if the Landlord does not require the Tenant to take a new lease pursuant to sub-paragraph (2) above the Tenant will pay to the Landlord on demand a sum equal to the Rents and other moneys that would have been payable under this Lease but for such determination disclaimer forfeiture or re-entry until the expiration of six months therefrom or until the premises shall have been re-let whichever shall first occur

(ii)   The liability of the Tenant hereunder shall not be affected by any neglect or forbearance of the Landlord in enforcing the payments of the Rents or the observance or performance of the said covenants and conditions or any refusal by the Landlord to accept rent at a time when the Landlord was entitled (or would after service of a notice under section 146 of the Law of Property Act 1925 have been entitled) to re-enter the premises or any variation of the terms of this Lease or any change in the constitution structure or powers of the Tenant the Assignee or the Landlord or any act which is beyond the powers of the Assignee or the surrender of part of the premises

(iii)   As between the Landlord and the Tenant the Tenant shall be deemed to be a principal debtor

(iv)   The Tenant shall not be entitled to participate in any security held by the Landlord in respect of the Assignee's obligations or stand in the Landlord's place in respect of such security

(v)   Where the Tenant is more than one person the release of one or more of them shall not release the others

(b)   That the Assignee shall covenant with the Landlord to pay the Rents reserved by and observe and perform the covenants and conditions on the part of the Tenant in this Lease

Rent deposit

THIS DEED made the   day of   One thousand nine hundred
and ninety
BETWEEN
(1)   whose registered office is at   ('the Landlord') and
(2)   whose registered office is at   ('the Tenant')
WITNESSES as follows

1   (1)   'the Landlord' means the person for the time being entitled to the
reversion immediately expectant on the term granted by the Lease
     (2)   'the Lease' means the Lease dated the   day of   199
and made between the Landlord (1) and the Tenant (2) and any deed or
document supplemental thereto
     (3)   'the Deposit' means the sum of (£   ) and any additional
amounts paid by way of rent deposit pursuant hereto and any part of such
amount or amounts from time to time in the Account
     (4)   'the Account' means the separate designated interest-bearing account
opened with a bank of the Landlord's choosing ('the Bank') or such other
account as the Landlord may in its absolute discretion select in which the
Deposit is lodged from time to time
     (5)   'a Permitted Assignment' is an assignment permitted by clause [   ]
of the Lease

2   The Landlord shall pay the Deposit into the Account and all interest
earned on the Deposit shall be for the benefit of the Tenant and shall be paid
to it in arrear within seven days of the same being credited to the Account
(and if so required by statute after deduction of tax for which the Landlord
shall account to the proper revenue authority) at such address as the Tenant
shall from time to time advise to the Landlord in writing

3   The Tenant hereby covenants and agrees with the Landlord as follows
     (1)   that if and whenever
     (a)   any rent or other payment due to the Landlord under the Lease is
not paid within fourteen days of the due date for payment (whether formally
demanded or not) or
     (b)   the Landlord becomes liable for any payment which should be
payable by the Tenant under the Lease and the Tenant shall not pay the same
within fourteen days of demand or
     (c)   the Landlord incurs any expenditure that is repayable to the
Landlord under the terms of the Lease and which is not repaid within
fourteen days of demand

then in any such case the Landlord may (without prejudice to its remedies under the Lease) withdraw from the Account for its own use and benefit such sum as may be required to satisfy any such rent or other payment or liability

(2) that in the event of any sum being withdrawn from the Account the Tenant shall within seven days of being notified of such event pay to the Bank for the credit of the Account a sum equivalent to the sum withdrawn

(3) that within fourteen days of determination of any rent review pursuant to the Lease the Tenant shall pay to the Bank for the credit of the Account a sum equivalent to [one quarter] of the difference between the annual rent prior to such review and the annual rent as reviewed plus value added tax thereon at the appropriate rate

(4) that any sum paid to the credit of the Account by the Tenant pursuant to sub-clause (2) or (3) above shall forthwith form part of the Deposit and be treated accordingly for the purposes of this Deed

(5) that the Deposit is and shall be charged to the Landlord as security for the performance of the Tenant's obligations under the Lease and this Deed

4   The Landlord shall forthwith upon making any withdrawal notify the Tenant within seven days of the amount of such withdrawal and of the circumstances justifying it

5   Subject as herein provided the Landlord shall release the Deposit or any remaining balance thereof to the Tenant within fourteen days of the happening of whichever of the following events shall first occur

(1) the expiry of the Term (as therein defined) of the Lease or

(2) the date of completion of a Permitted Assignment

PROVIDED THAT if on the date so provided for release there shall be a subsisting breach of any of the Tenant's obligations under the Lease the Landlord shall not be obliged to release the Deposit until fourteen days after such breach has been remedied

6   If the Lease is forfeited the Deposit shall continue to be available to the Landlord in the manner hereinbefore provided until it shall be exhausted or until there shall be no further liability of the Tenant to the Landlord whereupon any remaining balance of the Deposit shall forthwith be repaid to the Tenant

7   It is hereby agreed and declared

(1) that the breach of any of the obligations on the part of the Tenant contained in this Deed shall be deemed to be an event giving rise to the right of re-entry by the Landlord under the Lease

(2)   the Deposit shall at all times be and remain the property of the Tenant but subject to the charge hereinbefore set out

8   The Landlord's rights hereunder shall not be affected discharged or prejudiced in any way by any time given or any indulgence granted or other concession made by the Landlord to the Tenant and nothing herein contained shall prejudice or affect the obligations of the Tenant under the Lease

9   In this Deed where the context so admits words importing the singular number only shall include the plural number and vice versa and where two or more persons are included in the expression 'Landlord' or 'Tenant' obligations undertaken by such party shall be deemed to be joint and several

EXECUTED as a deed the day and year first above mentioned

THE COMMON SEAL of
was hereunto affixed in the presence of

          Director
          Secretary

SIGNED as a deed by the said
in the presence of
Witness
Address

Occupation

Clause to insert in a renewal lease under the Landlord and Tenant Act 1954

This Lease has been entered into pursuant to an order of the   Court (No.   ) made on the   day of   1995 and is not a new tenancy for the purposes of the Landlord and Tenant (Covenants) Act 1995.

Supplementary alienation agreement

THIS AGREEMENT is made the   day of   199
BETWEEN   (1)   of   ('the   Landlord')   and
(2)   of   ('the Tenant')
NOW IT IS AGREED as follows

1   In this agreement

1.1   'the Premises' means

1.2   'the Lease' means the lease of the Premises dated the   day
of   19   and made between (1)   and (2)

1.3   'the Landlord' includes the successors in title of the Landlord to the
Premises and any other person who is at any time entitled to the reversion
immediately expectant on the term of the Lease

1.4   'the Tenant' [includes] [does not include] successors in title of the
Tenant

1.5   'the Alienation Clause' means clause   in the Lease

1.6   'consent' includes licence

2   The Landlord and the Tenant agree that

2.1   the Landlord may withhold his consent to an assignment of the
Premises [or any part of them] under the Alienation Clause in [any of] the
circumstance[s] set out in the [first] schedule and that if he does so he shall
not be regarded as unreasonably withholding his consent

2.2   the Landlord may grant a consent to an assignment of the Premises or
any part of them under the Alienation Clause subject to any or all of the
conditions set out in the [second] schedule and that if he does so he shall not
be regarded as giving such consent subject to unreasonable conditions

AS WITNESS etc.

FIRST SCHEDULE
Circumstances in which consent may be withheld

SECOND SCHEDULE
Conditions subject to which consent may be granted

Rent review assumptions and disregards

Old leases

Assumption that the hypothetical lease will be a new lease

That the hypothetical lease is a new tenancy under section 1 of the Landlord and Tenant (Covenants) Act 1995

New leases

Assumption that the tenant does not require the landlord's consent to assign

That the hypothetical lease provides that the Tenant does not require the consent of the Landlord to assign this Lease

Assumption that the tenant is not required to enter into an authorised guarantee agreement

That the hypothetical lease provides that the Tenant is not required on an assignment of this Lease to enter into an authorised guarantee agreement

General assumption

That the hypothetical lease contains the same provisions as this Lease except the amount of rent, any rent-free period and the provisions in this Lease dealing with assignment

Disregards

Any effect on rent due to the fact that the Tenant's predecessor in title has entered into an authorised guarantee agreement

Any effect on rent due to the fact that this Lease requires the Tenant to enter into an authorised guarantee agreement on assignment of this Lease

Any effect on rent due to the conditions or restrictions on assignment contained in this Lease

Licence to assign with authorised guarantee agreement

1   THIS LICENCE by deed is made between the parties referred to in the Schedule supplemental to the Lease also referred to in it

2   The Lease contains a covenant by the Tenant not to assign the Premises without the consent of the Landlord

[3   The freehold reversion immediately expectant on the determination of the term created by the Lease is now vested in the Landlord]

[4   The Premises are now vested in the Tenant for all the residue of the term created by the Lease]

5   The Tenant desires to assign all his estate and interest in the Premises to the Assignee

6   The Landlord has agreed to grant the licence for such assignment upon the Assignee [and] the Tenant [and the Guarantor] covenanting as follows

NOW THIS DEED WITNESSETH as follows

1   In consideration of the following covenants by the Assignee [and] the Tenant [and the Guarantor] the Landlord grants to the Tenant licence to assign all the estate and interest of the Tenant in the Premises to the Assignee

2   In consideration of the preceding licence by the Landlord the Assignee covenants with the Landlord as follows

2.1   as from the date when the Tenant's estate and interest in the Premises shall be assigned to him the Assignee will pay the rent reserved by and observe and perform the covenants and conditions on the part of the Tenant contained in the Lease

2.2   to give notice of or register the assignment in accordance with the relevant terms of the Lease and to pay to the Landlord's solicitors a fee of £   plus VAT

2.3   if after the date of the assignment any sum or sums shall fall due for payment by the Tenant to the Landlord under the terms of the Lease in respect of any period before such date whether by way of rental or otherwise the Assignee shall pay such sum or sums to the Landlord forthwith upon their falling due

[3   In consideration of the preceding licence by the Landlord having been made at his request the Guarantor covenants with the Landlord as follows

3.1   the Assignee will pay the rents and other payments by the Lease reserved on the days and in manner stipulated in it and will perform and observe all the Tenant's covenants contained in the Lease and in case of default in such payment of rent or such other payment or in the performance or observance of such covenants the Guarantor will pay and make good to the Landlord on demand all losses damages costs charges and expenses arising or incurred by the Landlord as a consequence of such default

3.2   If for any reason the term created by the Lease shall be prematurely determined or a liquidator or trustee in bankruptcy of the Assignee disclaims the Lease or if the Lease shall otherwise be disclaimed in circumstances releasing the estate of the Assignee from liability or if this Lease is determined by forfeiture or re-entry and if within six months of any such event the Landlord shall by notice in writing so require the Guarantor will at the expense of the Guarantor enter into a new lease of the Premises for a term equal in duration to the residue remaining unexpired of the term granted by the Lease at the time of the grant of such lease to the Guarantor such lease to contain the like landlord's and tenant's covenants respectively and the like provisos and conditions in all respects (including the proviso for re-entry) as are contained in the Lease

3.3   If the Landlord does not require the Guarantor to take a new lease pursuant to clause 3.2 the Guarantor will pay to the Landlord on demand a sum equal to the rents and other moneys which would have been payable under this Lease but for such determination disclaimer forfeiture or re-entry until the expiration of [six months] therefrom or until the Premises shall have been re-let whichever shall first occur

3.4   The liability of the Guarantor hereunder shall not be affected by any neglect or forbearance of the Landlord in enforcing the payment of rent or the observance or performance of the said covenants and conditions or any refusal by the Landlord to accept rent at a time when the Landlord was entitled (or would after the service of a notice under section 146 of the Law of Property Act 1925 have been entitled) to re-enter the Premises or any variation of the terms of this Lease or any change in the constitution structure or powers of the Guarantor the Tenant or the Landlord or any act which is beyond the powers of the Tenant or the surrender of part of the Premises

3.5   As between the Landlord and the Guarantor the Guarantor shall be deemed to be a principal debtor

3.6   The Guarantor shall not be entitled to participate in any security held by the Landlord in respect of the Tenant's obligations or stand in the Landlord's place in respect of such security

3.7   Where the Guarantor is more than one person the release of one or more of them shall not release the others]

[4.1   The Tenant covenants with the Landlord that

(a)   the Assignee will pay the rents reserved and observe and perform its covenants and conditions in the Lease and the Tenant will indemnify the Landlord on demand against all losses damages costs and expenses arising out of any default by the Assignee

(b)   if for any reason the term created by the Lease shall be prematurely determined or a liquidator or a trustee in bankruptcy of the Assignee disclaims the Lease or if the Lease shall otherwise be disclaimed in circumstances releasing the estate of the Assignee from liability or if the Lease is determined by forfeiture or re-entry and if within six months of any such event the Landlord shall by notice in writing so require the Tenant will enter into a new lease of the Premises at the cost of the Tenant on the same terms for the residue of the term which would have remained had there been no such determination disclaimer forfeiture or re-entry

(c)   if the Landlord does not require the Tenant to take a new lease pursuant to sub-clause (b) above the Tenant will pay to the Landlord on demand a sum equal to the rent and other moneys that would have been payable under this Lease but for such determination disclaimer forfeiture or re-entry until the expiration of [six months] therefrom or until the Premises shall have been relet whichever shall first occur

4.2   The liability of the Tenant hereunder shall not be affected by any neglect or forbearance of the Landlord in enforcing payment of rent or observance or performance of the said covenants and conditions or any refusal by the Landlord to accept rent at a time when the Landlord was entitled (or would after service of a notice under section 146 of the Law of Property Act 1925 have been entitled) to re-enter the Premises or any variation of the terms of the Lease or any change in the constitution structure or powers of the Tenant the Assignee or the Landlord or any act which is beyond the powers of the Assignee or the surrender of part of the Premises

4.3   As between the Landlord and the Tenant the Tenant shall be deemed to be a principal debtor

4.4   The Tenant shall not be entitled to participate in any security held by the Landlord in respect of the Assignee's obligations or stand in the Landlord's place in respect of such security

4.5   Where the Tenant is more than one person the release of one or more of them shall not release the others]

5   In consideration of the grant by the Landlord of this Licence the Tenant covenants with the Landlord that the Tenant will pay the Landlord's

solicitors' and managing agents' charges and disbursements including VAT in connection with the preparation and completion of this deed and the counterpart of it and the stamp duty on it

6 Where any party hereto is two or more individuals obligations herein expressed or implied to be made by such party shall be deemed to be made by such individuals jointly and severally so as to apply and be enforceable against all both or any of such persons and their and each of their personal representatives

7 It is hereby agreed and declared

7.1 This Licence is restricted to the particular assignment authorised and the stipulations of the Lease shall remain in full force and effect

7.2 This Licence shall become void if such assignment is not completed before the expiry of three months from the date of this Licence

7.3 This Licence shall not prejudice the rights of the Landlord in respect of any breach (whether known to the Landlord or not) of the covenants agreements and conditions contained in the Lease and to be performed and observed on the part of the Tenant

EXECUTED as a deed the day and year first above mentioned

THE SCHEDULE

DATED the   day of   199

PARTIES
1 Landlord
2 Tenant
3 Assignee
4 Guarantor

LEASE
1 Date
2 Parties
3 Term
4 Initial Rent

PREMISES

THE COMMON SEAL of
was hereunto affixed in the presence of

THE COMMON SEAL OF
was hereunto affixed in the presence of

SIGNED AS A DEED by the said   in the presence of

Request for overriding lease

To: [name and address of landlord]

From: [name and address of the claimant]

Property: [address of property]

Lease dated:

and made between:

Qualifying Payment: [amount of payment]

Date:

Landlord and Tenant (Covenants) Act 1995, section 19

I/we give you notice that:

1.   I/we received from you on [insert date] a notice under section 17 of the Landlord and Tenant (Covenants) Act 1995.

2.   I/we now request that within a reasonable time of receiving this notice you grant to me/us an overriding lease in respect of the above property in accordance with section 19 of the said Act.

3.   The qualifying payment by which I/we am/are entitled to this lease is enclosed/was made to you on [insert date].

[Signed and dated]

Withdrawal of request for an overriding lease

To: [name and address of landlord]

From: [name and address of claimant]

Property: [address of property]

Date:

Landlord and Tenant (Covenants) Act 1995, section 19(9)(a)

I/we give you notice that:

1. By a notice dated the [insert date] I/we requested that you grant me/us an overriding lease in respect of the above property.

2. I/we today withdraw my/our request.

[Signed]

Index